THE SHEBOYGAN COUNTY
Connection

by Sheboygan County
Historical Research Center

Featuring articles previously seen in The Sheboygan Press

ISBN 978-0-9883759-6-3

Published by the Sheboygan County Historical Research Center, 518 Water Street Sheboygan Falls, WI 53085

schrc.org

All rights reserved
Printed in the United States of America

Published 2014

The Sheboygan County Connection

The Sheboygan County Connection deals with Sheboygan County residents and many of the unexpected and interesting ways they connect to national and worldwide events. From the Manhattan Project and the building of the Brooklyn Bridge to Dynamite Bill and the Beatles, county residents participate in the making of some really amazing history.

The columns seen here were originally run in the Sheboygan Press from February through October 2014. Extra information and added photos are also included. Make sure to check out the Dynamite Bill photos.

More information about each of the topics can be found at the Research Center. Many thanks to the Sheboygan Press and others who offered great information, images or ideas for these articles: Mary Joe Beniger, John and Eleanor Dees, Rich Dykstra, Mary Eckardt, Steve Gallimore, Jack Grandlic, Marilyn Hanson, Ed Harvey, Cedar Grove Holland Guild, Fred Horneck, Kathy Jeske, Ed Kaminsky, Kohler Co., Janice and Norb Kraemer, Carol Meyer, Mary Deeley Kunert, Don Lau, Tim and Steve Lawrence, Tom La Bouve, Huetta Manion, Mary Meyer, Angela Miller, Jim Mohr, Katie Reilly, Bob Spatt, Dick Stoelb, John Swart and so many more.

Table of Contents

Olympic Wear-Made in Sheboygan	7
If You Think This Winter Was Bad . . .	11
Fisheree Lore Runs Deep On County Lakes	15
We Are All Immigrants . . . Our Irish Ancestors	18
Rocky Knoll, Caring for Sheboygan County Citizens Since 1926	23
The Discovery of DNA Made Possible by a Sheboyganite?	27
Friendly Fire Incident; Two Minutes Early on the Trigger	29
Passenger Pigeons - From Abundance to Extinction	35
Skilled Town of Scott Cabinet Maker Donates Table to Lincoln	39
Break Out the Golf Clubs, Spring is Here	42
Thirty-One Years and a Lifetime Ago, the Death of H.C. Prange & Co.	47
Sheboygan Observes V-E Day, May 8, 1945	50
Harry Selfridge and his Wisconsin Connections	53
Sheboygan Calmly Greeted Halley's Comet	56
Plank Road Surveyor Paine Helped Build Brooklyn Bridge	59
Star Dusk Drive-In Provided 35 Years of Memories	63
The Golden Arches Arrived in 1958	67
Wisconsin's Beer Bar Phenomenon	71
Kiddies' Camp Serving the Community Since 1926	75
Rhine Center and its Screaming Eagle	79
Joyland, 1950s Summer Entertainment	83
Cedar Grove Celebrates Its Dutch Roots	86
Sheboygan County's Tenuous Ties to Public Enemy #1	90
The Sausage that Made Sheboygan Famous	94
A-fish-ianado: Helen Shaw was fly-fishing artist	101
Sheboygan County Supplied Scientists for Manhattan Project	106
Lost and Found in the Canadian Wilderness	111
In Our Spare Time: Bowling has been a Sheboygan Mainstay	115
Sheboygan County Meets the Fab Four	120
Falls' Helen Brainard Cole was notable Civil War Nurse	124
A Blasters' Blaster: The Legend of Dynamite Bill	128
WWII GIs bring pizza back to the states, Sheboygan	138
North to Alaska	145
Plymouth Rocks the County	149
Local Men Make History in Antarctica	153
An Uncommon Friendship	158
The Bubbler, Debunking the Myth	162
Friday Night Fish Fries	166
A Tale of Two Cows	171
Western People. . . Ballina, County Mayo	176

Olympic Wear
Made in Sheboygan

Anyone who watched the Olympic Games in the 1960s and 1970s saw a little bit of Sheboygan craftsmanship each time the U.S. Olympic Team was featured. Sheboygan-made clothing was worn by the athletes from the spectacular opening ceremonies to the celebratory closing of the games. Two Sheboygan manufacturers, Lakeland Manufacturing and Wigwam Mills, stepped up and provided coats, jackets, socks and knit hats to our athletes.

Lakeland Mfg. beat out the competition to win the right to make coats and jackets in 1964 and 1968. Wigwam Mills provided socks to the U.S. Nordic and Alpine ski teams, figure skaters and other winter sports participants from 1960 to 1972.

A Sheboygan Press article from February 18, 1963 boasted that Lakeland Manufacturing Company had been selected by the U.S. Olympic committee to make the official parade coat for the U.S. participants in the 1964 Winter Olympics at Innsbruck, Austria

The article continued to say that the Sheboygan manufacturer presented its fall styles in February of 1963 by the unique means of a musical ice show, "Parade of Champions, a Salute to the 1964 Olympic Games at Innsbruck." An audience of more than 450 of America's top retailers, fashion experts and members of the press and wire services viewed the show, featuring the premiere display of the 1964 Olympic parade coat. The coats were made in an off-white woolen fabric with a bulky knit shawl collar to match, edged in blue and red to tie in with the colors of the Olympic emblem.

Lakeland produced the sports coats here in its Sheboygan plant. In all, 150 of the Olympic Parade models were donated to the U.S. Olympic committee by the local firm.

Company Histories

Lakeland Manufacturing Company began in 1894 when H. J. Holman began the production of men's overalls. Herman Holman would go out and collect orders and, Sophia, his wife, would create them on her home sewing machine. The company grew and the clothing line added trousers, shirts and sports clothes for men and boys. In 1926, the company name was changed to Lakeland Manufacturing. Their old "Diamond" trademark was replaced with the new "Lakeland" label. The company moved into a new three story building at South 14th and Alabama. From the beginning there was an insistence on sturdy fabrics and fine workmanship. By 1979 the fourth generation of Holmans were producing more than 150,000 men's coats and jackets. Downturns in the economy plus foreign competition spelled the end for Lakeland in Sheboygan. The company closed in 1989 and was sold to a New York firm in 1990. Lakeland parade coats were worn by the U.S. Winter Olympics teams in 1964 in Innsbruck, Austria and 1968 in Grenoble, France. A travel jacket was used by the U.S. Olympic teams in the 1964 Tokyo and 1968 Mexico City Olympics.

Wigwam Mills began business as Hand Knit Hosiery in 1905. The first products were heavy woolen socks and liner mittens for lumbermen. Herbert Chesebro was the company president. A new building was built at the corner of 14th Street and Huron Avenue. The stock market crash of the 1920s and the following Great Depression took its toll on the hosiery business, but with the help of a local bank, the company stayed in business. During WWII Handknit Hosiery devoted 75% of its production to heavy wool socks for the Army. On January 1, 1957 the company changed its name to Wigwam Mills, Inc. and in 1969 the company relocated to its Crocker Avenue facility. In 1968 Wigwam supplied socks to U.S. skaters for the Grenoble, France winter games. Peggy Fleming won a gold medal for figure skating that year. In 1972 Wigwam supplied socks and knit hats to the U.S. ski teams for the Sapporo, Japan games where Barbara Cochran became the first U.S. gold medalist in skiing in two decades when she won the women's slalom.

At left: Parade coat worn by the U.S. Olympic Team during the opening ceremonies of the 1964 Winter Games in Innsbruck, Austria designed and manufactured in Sheboygan by Lakeland Mfg. Company.

Lakeland Label in 1964 Parade Coat used in Innsbruck, Austria.

Wigwam Mills Company Logo

Herman and Sophia Holman

Frankfurt, Germany, January, 1964: Six members of the U.S. figure skating team strike a one-legged pose in front of the plane on which they just arrived from New York on their way to the Winter Olympics at Innsbruck, Austria. They are, left to right, Albertina Noyes, Tommy Litz, Christie Haigler, Monty Hoyt, Peggy Fleming and Scott Allen. Beneath the levity of the photo, though, was an undercurrent of sadness; since the last Olympics, the entire U.S. team had perished in a plane crash in Belgium in 1961. Allen, only 14 years old, sparked the rebuilding effort with a bronze medal at Innsbruck; four years later, Fleming captured a gold at Grenoble.

1968 Winter Games– Grenoble, France

U.S. figure skaters in red parade coats. Left to right: Tina Noyes, Janet Lynn Nowiki and Peggy Fleming.

If You Think This Winter Was Bad . . .

As the winter of 2013-2014 marches on, and we dream of spring, let's revisit two historic winters.

The winter of 1880-1881 was brutal. In October 1880, sleet, snow and 125-mph winds swept through the area. One of the Great Lakes' legendary shipwrecks, the sinking of the steamer, Alpena, took place on Lake Michigan and killed 75 passengers. The cruel weather continued into the early part of 1881. The storm of February 2-4 brought 36 inches of snow that drifted 'like great ocean waves of 18 feet or higher'. Two hundred shovelers worked to dig out the city of Sheboygan. It would take days to do so. On Eighth Street, they dug tunnels through drifts between streets and stores. A train was stuck midway between Sheboygan and Sheboygan Falls for two weeks with just its smokestack visible." At one time during the great storms the snow turned to a heavy rain which saturated the top of the snow. This was followed by freezing weather that stopped the drifting but created a thick, solid crust nearly impossible to move.

The greatest depth of snow and the greatest hardship for passenger traffic was between February 26th and March 28th during which time the snow, wind and sometimes rain storms seemed to do their utmost to tie up all trains and make country highways impassable. The high winds during the brief periods between storms filled all the cuts nearly as fast as armies of shovelers could clear the tracks. Snow that year would not disappear fully until July.

The winter of 1936 remains the one to surpass. Three heavy snowstorms hit the county in a little over two weeks that year, on January 22, February 3 and February 8, 1936. Snowfall measured 56 inches in Plymouth. And when it wasn't snowing, gale force winds shifted the snow into stunning new configurations. Some county roads were blocked until March. Farmers got their milk and eggs to market by bobsled, but they had to guide their horses carefully so the animals didn't trip on telephone lines that barely stretched above the 24-foot snow drifts.

Four people were marooned at Riverdale Golf Club, unsuccessfully calling airports to see if someone could fly over and drop food. Along with the snow and wind, temperatures stayed well below normal, nights hitting 20 below zero. Lake Michigan froze over for the first time in 30 years.

At daybreak on Thursday, February 18, 1936, seven Coast Guardsmen risked their lives to save the crew of an icebound fishing tug, the R.K. Smith, stranded 1 ½ miles off Sheboygan's north pier. That winter, area fishermen estimated they lost over a quarter million dollars because they were unable to penetrate the frozen expanse of Lake Michigan.

After three days with no mail delivery, Sheboygan Press Editor Charles Broughton, used his clout to get the mail moving. Trucks didn't work so he telegraphed the Postmaster General, James Farley, asking that the interurban lines be used for sending mail. The trains used rotary plows attached to the front end to make their way. It was often necessary to send a crew on ahead to knock down the biggest drifts.

Compassion was shown for the seagulls and other birds that were dying of starvation, their food sources buried beneath snow and ice. City workers began carting loads of garbage to the lakefront and dumping it, rather than burning it as usual."

Maurice "Red" Hughes of Plymouth, who worked for the Sheboygan County Highway Department in 1936, remembered that winter well. "The County didn't have much equipment at that time. There were three Liberty trucks. The top speed was 15 mph. We had a Clintonville four-wheel drive truck and a Monarch 60H crawler-type tractor. We hooked two and three Liberty trucks together at that time. By the time the last town roads were opened in March, Sheboygan County had a power shove

Cascade resident, Art Vanderkin, also worked out of the Cascade shed in 1936. He reported that, "the Liberty trucks we had were from WWI. One had pneumatic tires and the others had hard rubber tires. It was difficult keeping chains on them. There were no heated cabs and just side curtains. To keep the windshield open we used a salt sack. To operate the plow a crank came in below the windshield that you used to wind the cable. They pushed the snow like a bulldozer, didn't roll it off to the side like now

Both men stayed at the shed for much of two weeks. Vanderkin recalls farmers blinking their porch lights at him when he was out plowing after midnight, beckoning him in for a hot meal. Another time Vanderkin and a fellow worker were stranded on Hwy. V near Parnell. He called his foreman, Herb Bartel, for help. Help was a long time in coming. The men stayed in their truck as long as they could. When it got too cold, they went to a nearby barn to stay, the heat from the cows keeping them warm. They were rescued the next afternoon.

Finally, in March, the county Highway Committee called a special meeting and purchased two crawlers RD8 95-horsepower Caterpillar tractors with "V" plows- the kind the U.S. Army used in WWII to build the Military Supply Route to Alaska. Each county shed also got a new truck. They ran day and night until the cleanup was completed.

As long and cold as this winter has been, be glad it's not 1936. Visit the Research Center to learn more about those historic winter storms.

County employees clearing roads north of Parnell.

The Chicago and Northwestern Railway's big rotary plow as it was heading north to Sheboygan from Cedar Grove.

County worker, Art Vanderkin, with one of the new V-plows purchased after 1936.

February 2, 1908- Random Lake. Train was nine hours late due to storm. Photo courtesy of the Random Lake Area Historical Society.

Fisheree Lore Runs Deep on County Lakes

FISHEREE. Dictionaries don't even recognize it as a word, yet we Wisconsinites know exactly what it means. It means ice fishing and fun, a chance to breathe the cold, clean winter air, to spend time outdoors with family and friends, and to relax, perhaps, with a twelve ounce cold one.

As we enter the first weeks of March, the annual fisherees are done for 2014 and the shanties and trucks must come off the county's still ice-covered lakes within days. But happily, the colossal fish stories remain and the enthusiasm for next year begins to build almost immediately. But what do we really know about the history of ice fishing and fisherees?

Wisconsin ranks second nationally in fishing popularity and that certainly doesn't change as winter seals the lakes under ice. Ice anglers catch 14 million fish across the United States during the winter fishing season. This winter of 2013-2014, when the ice deepened to more than 3 feet, has been an outstanding year.

Sheboygan County ice fishing traditions run deep on many of its seventy-two lakes. Fisherees are held annually on Lake Ellen at Cascade and Crooked and Long Lakes on the Fond du Lac County line. There is also the Four Lakes Fisheree sponsored by the Crystal Lake Sportsman's Club, which involves Crystal, Little Elkhart and Elkhart Lakes and the Sheboygan Marsh. Thousands of people participate in the fishing contests every year.

Ice fishing in Wisconsin dates back to well before the arrival of European settlers when American Indians chopped holes in the ice in order to spear fish to supplement their winter diets, but was virtually non-existent among European settlers until the 1880s. Even then it took the lean years of the Great Depression to bring it into the mainstream. The first fisherees or large scale fishing contests started in the 1950s and 1960s. Curiously the term 'fisheree' seems to be a regionalism used predominantly in the Upper Midwest, but most commonly in Wisconsin.

Throughout Wisconsin during the cold winter months, frozen lakes are dotted with fishermen and their ice shanties. Historically, two basic tools have been used to make holes in the ice, the spud and the auger. A spud is a rod used to chip a hole in the ice that isn't very thick. An auger is a corkscrew-like device with a cutting blade that operates like a drill to make a hole in the ice. This is where Sheboygan County meets ice fishing and the fisheree. The most common ice auger found on Midwest lakes is the Jiffy Ice Auger produced by Feldmann

Manufacturing and Engineering of Sheboygan Falls. It is frequently the prize for the biggest fish at local derbies.

The origin of the power ice drill began in 1948. A friend of Marvin Feldmann's, who loved to ice fish, but dreamed of never again having to hand-turn an auger through two feet of ice approached Marvin to craft a product that could cut through ice quickly and easily. Feldmann designed a gear box and clutch that would let a two-cycle engine power an oversized drill bit.

Marvin's invention went through a number of iterations before he succeeded in developing a product that could cut through the ice, with engine power, in a reasonable fashion, but by 1951 the Jiffy Power Ice Drill came into being. Fifty were produced that first year. Today, Feldmann Manufacturing produces around 20,000 units per year. The machines have become more powerful and lighter through improved technology, but remain the industry leader.

Gone are the days of the overturned bucket, the willow fishing rod and hand drill, replaced by sonar and GPS and deluxe fish shanties, but the camaraderie and appreciation of Mother Nature's winter beauty remains. Next year why don't you try a fisheree? It might be fun!

The Sheboygan County Historical Research Center has very little information on ice fishing in the county. We would love to have you share what you know about the topic. Photos, posters, stories, etc. are wanted and the older the better.

This ice shanty photo was taken in the mid-1920s. The 6' bar between the shovel and the axe is a "spud" used with the axe to make the hole in the hole in ice and the pole coming from the top of the shanty is likely a "pickerel spear".

Inventor, Marvin Feldmann and one of his early Jiffy Ice Drills. This image was taken about 1950 on the Walter Hueppchen farm in Plymouth.

With rough going and poor fishing at Lake Winnebago in January of 1962, more ice fishermen were trying their luck on local lakes. At one point fifty cars dotted the ice, seen here, at Crystal Lake in Sheboygan County. The perch were running very well at Crystal and catches ran as high as fifty per man on good days. the ice was approximately 20 inches in depth at the time.

We Are All Immigrants . . . Our Irish Ancestors

This time of the year we are all Irish, if just for a moment. As we head toward another St. Patrick's Day, it is only fitting that we honor our ancestors for their sacrifices and remember we are all immigrants. Whether our forbears arrived here in the 1790s or the 1840s, each of our families brought pieces of an old culture and made contributions to a new one.

Many first generation immigrants maintained their old ways of life and languages until their deaths, but their children did not. The second generation learned English easily and sought American lifestyles. Old ways diminished or mingled with the new, creating, once again, a different type of American adding to the ever evolving melting pot, or as we call it in my family, our ethnic smorgasbord.

The first Irish settlers in America were the Scotch-Irish. After the American Revolution, some 250,000 left Ireland for North America entering through New York or Philadelphia. They were Protestants whose families had originally lived in Scotland or northern England and been part of earlier plantations to Ireland.

Between 1850 and 1900 another 2.9 million poverty stricken Irish Catholics left. Forced out by starvation, eviction and disease the population of Ireland dropped by more than one-third. Immigration abroad exploded. People fled to live. And where did these Irish go? The majority came to America.

Sheboygan County is home to many of those immigrant Irish families. More than 600 families settled in a broad swath from the town of Lima west to the town of Byron in Fond du Lac County. Those 600 families amounted to more than 6000 people of Irish descent.

Immigrant families spoke little of their reasons for leaving their native land. They skipped the gory details of escape from famine, disease and poverty, things that at the same time horrified and embarrassed them. Here we honor a handful of families by telling their stories.

Daniel and Bridget Flannery Heraty fled their home in the Parish of Aughagower, County Mayo, Ireland in 1847. The potato crop had failed for the second year and the hungry months would soon be on them again. They survived an outbreak of smallpox in their townland of Doon. The large Heraty family, three generations of them, sailed on the famine ship Manchester departing from Liverpool, arriving 13 July 1847. As they neared their destination of Quebec baby Martin died from typhoid. Mother Bridget, horrified by the thought of a burial at sea, kept him hidden in the folds of her skirt until they reached land. He was buried on banks of the St. Lawrence River, perhaps at Grosse Ile. Their journey's end was the town of Mitchell where they bought land and educated their children.

Thomas Blackstock was a "rags to riches" figure straight out of a book. A city leader and philanthropist, Blackstock was born in 1834 in County Armagh in the north of Ireland. Penniless, he joined relatives here in 1849. His classmates at Union School teased him about his old clothes, but one day his principal, Hector Ross, gave the boys a bawling out for teasing for teasing Tom. He told them, "You should be ashamed of yourselves because of your extreme rudeness; His clothing may not be as modern as those you are privileged to wear, but I predict that the day will come when this boy will amount to more than anyone of you who now torment him." Blackstock was ambitious and successful serving as a three-term mayor of Sheboygan and president of Phoenix Chair.

Even though Michael Deeley was born in London his ancestral home was County Limerick. Michael came to America with his parents, David and Honora O'Grady Deeley, when he was eleven months old in 1867. Moving frequently to follow work in New England, Michael began his career in the woolen mills. By age sixteen he was supervising the carding rooms. In 1889, he was recruited by the Brickner Woolen Mills in Sheboygan Falls to be Boss Carder. Deeley spent the next forty-four year working hard and making a great life for his Irish-American kids.

The vast Kennedy clan hailed from Powers Court, County Wicklow. John and Margaret McGraw Kennedy and their family faced tragedy as they left Ireland in 1830. Margaret died aboard ship giving birth to daughter, Ann, and was buried at sea. The grieving family landed in Quebec and walked 183 miles on the Old Canada Road to Skowhegan, Maine where they lived until they settled in Wisconsin in 1874 at Five Corners in the town of Lima and flourished.

Larry and Maggie Farley O'Reilly, my second great-grandparents, were married for just one day when they left Ireland forever with his family. Imagine what Maggie's family must have felt, watching their daughter leave, knowing they'd never see her again? The group walked 30 miles to Dublin, crossed the Irish Sea to Liverpool and six weeks later, in June of 1844, they were in New York City. Luckily they all spoke English, and they knew enough to escape the city. The family made its way to Cold Spring, just across the Hudson from West Point, where the men earned enough money to go west to Mitchell, Wisconsin and buy land- 320 glorious acres – all theirs. No rent due. No fear of eviction.

Whether our ancestors came for economic reasons or for greater freedom, they ultimately came for a better life, a chance to raise a family and a chance to make something of themselves. Their lives and their journeys were not for the faint of heart. They were not journeys easily taken.

So in this season of Irish festivity, let us also remember those who came before us and the hardships they endured, and celebrate the fact that we are all immigrants.

The Thomas and Mary Ann Scanlan Heraty homestead in the town of Mitchell, above. Heraty's family came from County Mayo in 1847 escaping a small pox epidemic and the great potato famine.

Thomas Blackstock came from County Armagh as a teenager and prospered to become president of the Phoenix Chair Company.

Thomas Blackstock's gravestone in Calvary Cemetery, Sheboygan, Wisconsin.

A business advertisement for the business of Thomas Blackstock, Drugs and Books.

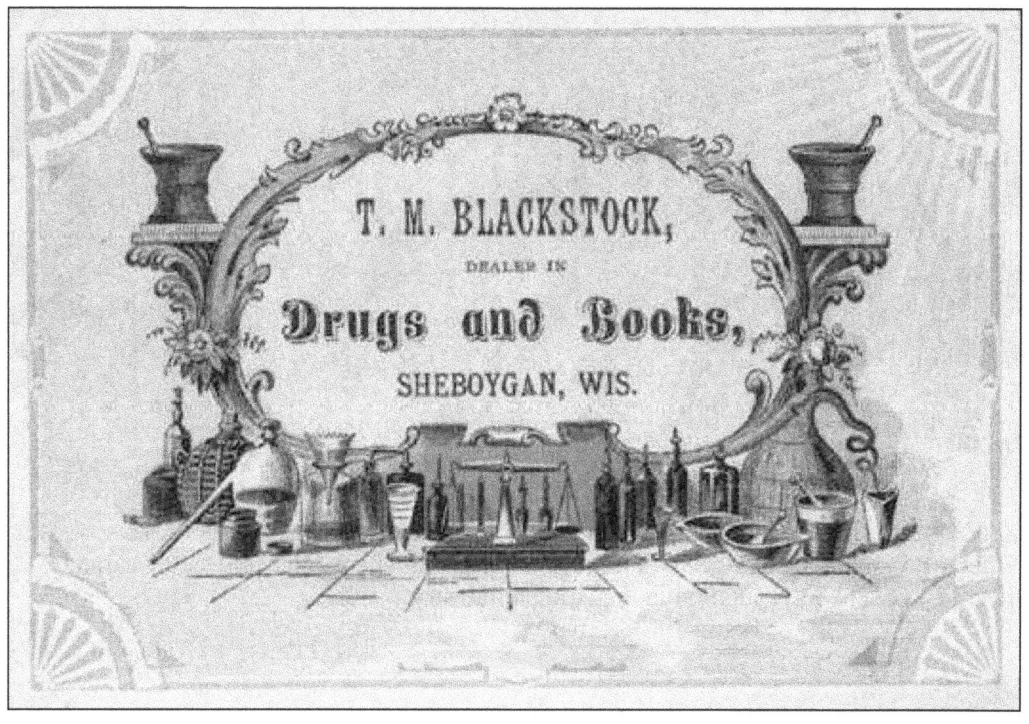

Michael Deeley with his daughter Margaret circa 1900.

Brickner Woolen Mills, Sheboygan Falls, Wisconsin, where Michael Deeley earned a living and made his reputation in the woolen industry.

Rocky Knoll,
Caring for Sheboygan County Citizens Since 1926

Each March 24th we note World TB Day, a day designed to remind the public that the scourge that once affected so many in Sheboygan County remains an epidemic in much of the world. It commemorates the day in 1882 when Dr. Robert Koch announced that he had discovered the cause of tuberculosis, the TB bacillus. At that time TB was raging through Europe and the Americas, causing the death of one out of every seven people.

Sheboygan County wasn't immune from this terrible disease; Its citizens suffered mightily and in large numbers. A facility was much needed for patient treatment. That facility was Rocky Knoll.

When Rocky Knoll opened its doors in 1926, it was the most technologically advanced and best staffed tuberculosis sanatorium in the state. It was described as possibly the best treatment center to be found anywhere in the country. E.A. Stubenrauch of Sheboygan was the architect for the project.

According to newspaper accounts at the time of its dedication, it had a fumigating machine and an x-ray machine, nearly unheard of in the 1920s. It also had state-of- the-art dust control, which meant rounded metal corners and terrazzo floors — easy to clean. Sun cure porches, used for sleeping in all types of weather, framed the front façade of the building.

The original plan was for a 40-bed hospital, but before the project began it was apparent that so many people in Sheboygan County were infected with TB that the facility would have to double in size. By the end of 1926 the 80 beds were already filled.

TB became an issue in 1921 when "chest clinics" revealed there were already 85 cases of tuberculosis in the county. This number did not include the 34 patients in other counties or servicemen in government hospitals.

The site for Rocky Knoll was chosen because of the need for isolated community life. Isolation suited the general public as well. Sheboygan County was a sympathetic place for TB treatment. It was not uncommon in some areas of the East to buy a TB patient a one-way ticket to Arizona, Colorado or California. Those dry climates of the west were considered better for tuberculosis patients, but the on-way ticket was a rather inhumane way of ridding the area of a difficult problem. Sheboygan County rose to the occasion and learned to treat patients effectively and with compassion.

Children afflicted with the disease were also taken to Rocky Knoll. They were separated from their friends and all but immediate family for long periods of time. There was a special ward with a large play area and classroom, along with rooms with sun cure porches. When it was determined children were well enough to risk sending them home, they went first to a special school in Sheboygan—the Fresh Air School which opened in 1918 at the Third Ward School on South Eighth Street. In 1931, the Fresh Air School moved to Longfellow School.

In 1800 tuberculosis killed more people than cancer or heart disease. In 1906 the mortality schedule listed 110 deaths from TB, but by 1926 only 60 deaths were reported. Rest, fresh air, cod liver oil and sunshine were the only known treatments. The death toll continued until 1944 when the development of streptomycin made TB a treatable and curable disease, not a death sentence.

In a September 1955 Sheboygan Press article, the title proclaims, "Board Favors Use of Rocky Knoll for Aged". One wing of Rocky Knoll Tuberculosis Sanatorium was to be set aside for the care of aged and infirm persons who were bed-ridden. Beginning January 1, 1956 patients were admitted on a voluntary basis, but the article states that "in no way was the dwelling to be used for people able to get around and take care of themselves."

An October 28, 1962 Sheboygan Press headline announces, TB Down, But Hospital Care of Aged Goes On. The article states, "While the treatment of tuberculosis has changed to such an extent that a large number of beds is no longer necessary, there remains need of beds for the chronically ill and aged at Rocky Knoll Sanitarium and Hospital."

Treatment for tuberculosis patients had changed so much by 1962 that the sanatorium wing of Rocky Knoll was rarely filled to capacity. The patient load varied between 45 and 65 over a year. Over the course of the decade of the 1960s, the focus of Rocky Knoll became the elderly and chronically ill.

Still a county-owned facility, Rocky Knoll in 2014 specializes in the care of the elderly, patients with special needs, cognitive and physical, Alzheimer's patients and those in need of short-term rehabilitation. The facility and its staff have professionally served the needs of the residents of Sheboygan County, providing a caring home to the most vulnerable of our residents.

Rocky Knoll in 1926 at the time of its grand opening as a Tuberculosis Sanitorium. The facility is north of Plymouth on Highway 67.

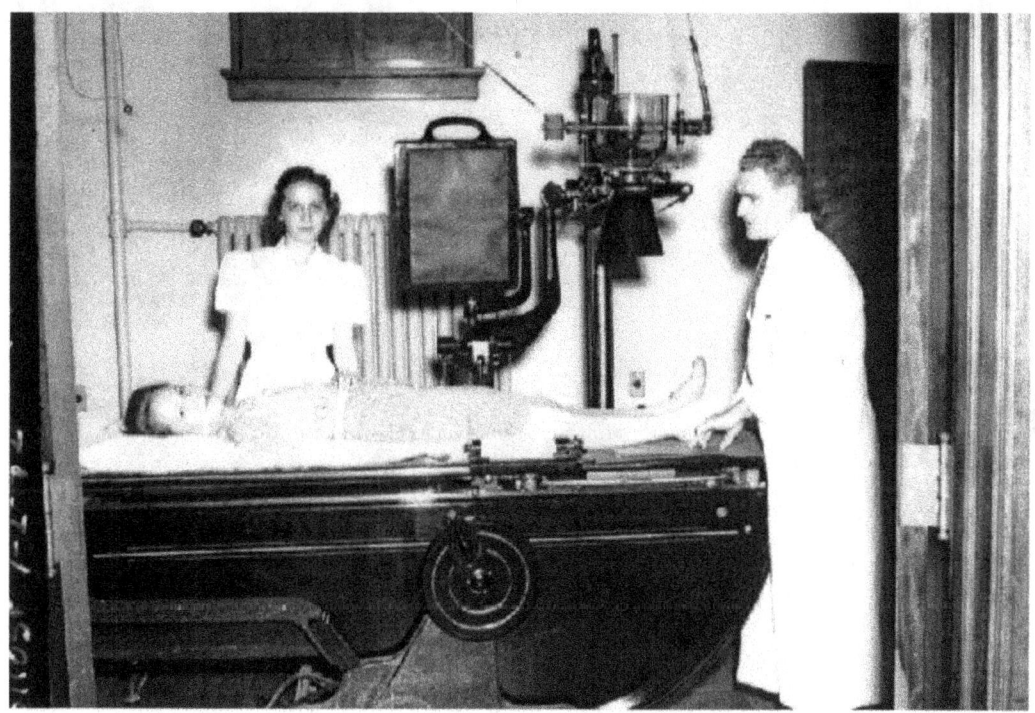
A patient is treated using the latest in x-ray equipment at Rocky Knoll seen here on July 7, 1942.

Rocky Knoll Christmas. December 18, 1934. TB patients decorate their Christmas tree.

The Discovery of DNA Made Possible by a Sheboyganite?

The discovery of the structure of DNA was reported sixty-one years ago this month and remarkably Sheboygan County has an essential connection to that breakthrough.

We all know that lions only give birth to lion cubs, cows to calves, dogs to puppies and so on for every type of living creature, but do we know how and why that occurs? The answer lies in a molecule called deoxyribonucleic acid (DNA), which contains the biological instructions that make each species unique.

A German biochemist, Frederich Miescher, first observed DNA in the late 1800s. But nearly a century passed from that discovery until researchers unraveled the structure of the DNA molecule and realized its central importance to biology.

Now you ask, how is this connected to Sheboygan County? Well, on April 25, 1953, a ground breaking paper appeared in the scientific journal Nature in which James Watson and Francis Crick, scientists at Cambridge, reported the discovery of the structure of DNA - the molecule from which all genes are made.

Crick and Watson used model building to reveal the now famous double helix of DNA, but they had struggled for years to get it right. It wasn't until theoretical and physical chemist, Jerry Donohue, pointed out in the spring of 1953 that they were using the wrong structures for the nitrogen bases, and that a different scenario for the structures would form the needed hydrogen bonds. With that valuable contribution Watson and Crick soon after discovered the famous double-helix of DNA.

DNA's discovery has been called the most important biological work of the last 100 years, and the field it opened may be the scientific frontier for the next 100. In 1962, Watson and Crick won the Nobel Prize for physiology/medicine because of this DNA research.

Jerry Donohue III was born on June 12, 1920 in Sheboygan, Wisconsin, the son of Jerry Donohue, of Donohue Engineering fame, and Leila Marian Bishop. A 1937 graduate of Sheboygan High School he received his Bachelors (1941) and Masters (1943) degrees from Dartmouth College. He earned his Ph.D. in 1947 at the California Institute of Technology under Linus Pauling, one of the most influential chemists of the 20th century.

Throughout his life Donohue's research focused on crystal structures and hydrogen-bonding. In 1952, he was given a Guggenheim Foundation grant to study at Cambridge University in England for 6 months. Interestingly, while at Cambridge Donohue shared an office with Francis Crick and James D. Watson.

From 1959 to 1960, Donohue, accompanied by his wife, Patricia Schreier Donohue, and two children, Terrance and Nora, spent a year at the Swiss Federal Institute of Technology in Zurich, Switzerland studying applications of quantum mechanics.

In 1962, Donohue was named Assistant Professor of Chemistry at the University of Southern California where he continued to specialize in hydrogen-bonding. In 1966, Donohue joined the chemistry faculty of the University of Pennsylvania as the Rhodes-Thompson Professor of Chemistry.

Jerry Donohue III retired from his Penn position because of ill-health in 1985, and died that same year from cancer at the age of 65. He was survived by his wife, Patricia Schreier, also a native of Sheboygan and their two children, Terrence and Nora.

Donohue's papers are housed at Pennsylvania University's Archive and Records Center. You can see his correspondence with Crick and Watson online at http://profiles.nlm.nih.gov/ps/access/SCBBND.pdf.

You can also find more information on Jerry Donohue and other famous Sheboygan County residents at the Sheboygan County Historical Research Center.

Professor Jerry Donohue III of Penn University discussing his contribution to the 1953 discovery of DNA.

Friendly Fire Incident; Two Minutes Early on the Trigger

On Monday, evening, March 17, 1958, a RB-47 reconnaissance bomber made a gunnery practice run over the Air Force gunnery range located about twenty-five miles southeast of Sheboygan, Wisconsin over Lake Michigan.

The sun had set at 6:00 p.m. It was overcast and by 6:45 p.m. it was dark when three homes in Sheboygan County were hit by 20mm cannon bullets from the tail guns of the RB-47 bomber. The bomber made its gunnery run from the southeast to the northwest and made a left turn over the Sheboygan Falls-Oostburg area in preparation of flying back to its base in Ohio.

For some undisclosed reason the 20mm cannon guns on the plane fired over land, resulting in bullets hitting homes and pavement in Sheboygan Falls and Oostburg, while two empty spent shell casings landed in a barn yard about one mile northeast of Hingham, Wisconsin. At the speed that the B-47 bomber was making the left hand turn north of Oostburg, this incident would not have occurred if the co-pilot who was in control of the 20mm cannons on the RB-47, would have waited just two minutes before firing the two bursts of twenty shells each. It is possible that the firings were due to mechanical issues, but based on the actions taken by the Air Force against the crew it most probably was human error by the co-pilot.

According to the information provided by the Air Force, at the time, the bomber was flying at an altitude of 36,000 feet, and the twin 20mm cannons on the RB-47, normally, fire in bursts of twenty shells at a time. Probably, firing ten shells from each gun, during the twenty shell burst. The bomber had a top speed of 600 miles per hour and was probably cruising at about 400 miles per hour while on the practice run over the gunnery range. If the firing of the cannons in the tail gun turret on the bomber had occurred two minutes later all of the ordnance would have fallen into Lake Michigan and it would have been a non-event.

Since the residents of the homes in Sheboygan Falls feel that the bullets came from the southwest, it is possible that the casings found in Hingham were from the burst fired toward Sheboygan Falls as the plane made its turn. The casings would follow in the direction of the plane while the bullets were fired in the opposite direction from the tail of the plane. The bullet that hit the Oostburg home appeared to come from the southeast and may have been one bullet, of a second burst of twenty shells, while the plane was over Lake Michigan with the shell casings falling in Lake Michigan. The Theune home was on the north side of Oostburg and it is very likely that the nineteen other bullets landed in farm fields on the north side of Oostburg.

All of the known recovered bullets were painted blue, indicating that they were practice rounds, and turned over to the Air Force for evaluation and ballistic testing, while the spent shell casings were not reported until now.

Fortunately, no one was injured in this incident. The Air Force was very sensitive to public relations at this time since one week prior to this "Friendly Fire" incident another Air Force bomber had dropped an unarmed atomic bomb over South Carolina, injuring six people.

While this incident occurred fifty-six years ago, all three of the homes hit by the friendly fire remain in the same configuration externally, as they were in 1958. The three families whose homes were hit in this incident were: Francis and Mary Deeley of 127 Pinehurst Court, Sheboygan Falls; the John and Geri Novotny family of 651 Leavens also of Falls; and the Lloyd and Harriet Theune home at Wisconsin and 10th Streets in Oostburg.

This story was investigated and written by John Swart of Oostburg. There is more to the story and it's available at The Research Center. John is a great SCHRC researcher and volunteer.

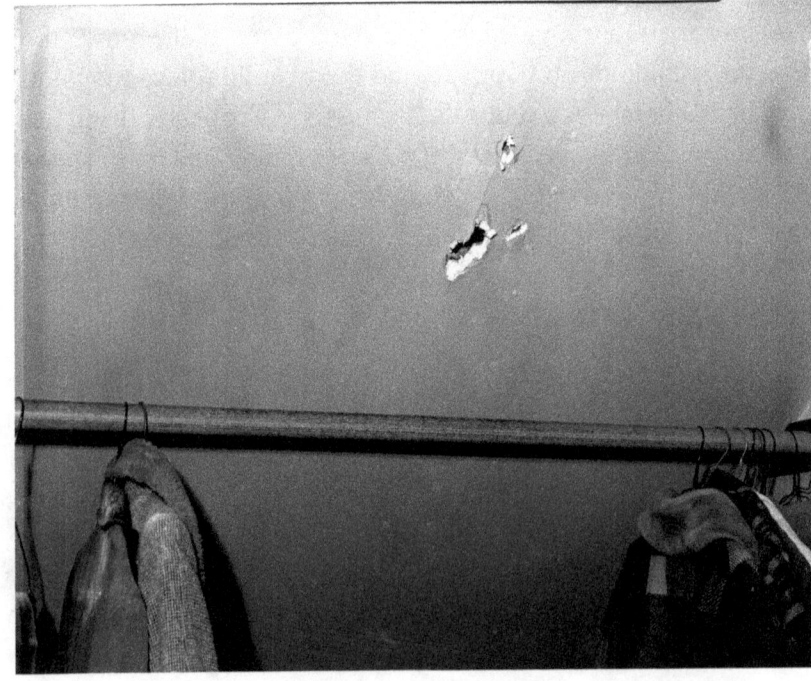

A stray bullet hole in the wall of a closet in the Deeley home, Sheboygan Falls.

A 20mm apparently fired from an airplane came through the roof and a ceiling at the John Novotny home in Sheboygan Falls Monday evening broke two year old Sally Novotny's piggy bank, then gouged the hole in the wall. Sally is holding the piggy bank broken by the large bullet, Sister Judy, 4, is at left and sister, Diane, 5, is at right. The bullet hole is just above where Sally's crib stood the week before.

Bullets recovered from the strafing event are examined by officials.

Below: Air Force investigators at Novotny's in Sheboygan Falls.

At left: Investigators meet in the Sheriff's office to examine the evidence found after the strafing of March 17, 1958.

Holland Evening Sentinel - Holland, Michigan - March 19, 1958

Air Force Admits Firing Of Shells

Sheboygan, Wis. (UP) - A congressman today demanded the Air Force stop armed training fights near urban areas as a result of the accidental strafing of two communities by a B47 jet bomber.

Rep. William K. Van Pelt (R - Wis.) told Air force Secretary James H. Douglas that lives were endangered when 20-millimeter cannon shells ripped three homes and spattered streets Monday night at nearby Sheboygan Falls and Oostburg.

Last week, other congressmen issued similar demands when an unfused atomic bomb accidentally dropped from a B47 at Florence, S.C., injuring six persons.

An Air Force investigating team rushed to the Sheboygan area Tuesday and confirmed that the shells came from a Lockbourne Air Force Base bomber on a routine gunnery training mission.

Brig. Gen. Donald W. Saunders of the Strategic Air Command base at Westover, Mass., and head of the investigating team, theorized the shells left the bomber's cannon after it had left the Lake Michigan firing range.

However, he said further investigation was needed to determine the cause of the gun's malfunctioning. Ordinarily, the cannon fires 20 shells in a burst and not one shell at a time.

Saunders said the plane stopped firing six miles before it cleared the gunnery range 25 miles south east of Sheboygan.

No one was injured in the strafing which sent about five or six shells into the two communities.

The shells started fires in two homes when they exploded.

Salisbury Times - Salisbury Maryland - March 18, 1958 Cannon Shells Rip Roofs In Wisconsin City

Sheboygan Falls, Wis. (AP) - Explosive cannon shells whipped out of the sky last night, pelting streets and hammering into at least three houses.

No one was injured, but residents of the area were warned to be on the lookout for any other shells which might be unexploded.

The blue-tipped projectiles were identified as shells from a 20 mm cannon mounted on American military aircraft.

Came From B47

Capt. Robert Dietz, Air Force information officer at Chicago's O'Hare Field, said he was informed the shells came from a B47 based at Lockbourne Air Force Base near Columbus, Ohio.

At Lockbourne AFB, Lt. Billy Baxter, an information officer, said the only Lockbourne plane over Wisconsin last night was an RB47 which did not have ammunition in its tail cannon, the only armament it carries.

The RB47 is a camera-equipped version of the six-jet B47 bomber.

Lt. Baxter said the 26th Strategic Reconnaissance Wing has one RB47 flying in "that general direction," but he said it was not scheduled to arrive in this area until after the cannon fire occurred.

Roofs Are Pierced

Projectiles pierced the roofs of the John Novotny house here, the home of Lloyd Theune at nearby Oostburg and the residence of Francis Deeley, Sheboygan Falls.

Police Chief Henry Dillmann of Sheboygan Falls said one shell exploded about 20 yards ahead of his car on Highway 23.

Officer Thomas Winter said other shells exploded in the street here.

Passenger Pigeons – From abundance to extinction

2014 marks the one hundredth anniversary of the extinction of the passenger pigeon. Once the most plentiful land bird on earth it went from abundance to extinction in a period of about fifty years.

When Europeans began exploring North America in the 17th and 18th centuries historians estimate there were 3 to 5 billion passenger pigeons. Yes, that really is billion. They made up, perhaps, 40 percent of the total North American bird population. Each spring flocks migrated from the South to the Midwest, making the return journey in the fall, darkening the sky with their passing. A flight over Columbus, Ohio, in 1855 prompted the following eye-witness account: "As the watchers stared, the hum increased to a mighty throbbing. Now everyone was out of the houses and stores, looking apprehensively at the growing cloud, which was blotting out the rays of the sun. Children screamed and ran for home. Women gathered their long skirts and hurried for the shelter of stores. Horses bolted. A few people mumbled frightened words about the approach of the millennium, and several dropped on their knees and prayed."

Passenger pigeons would fly and nest as huge groups. John James Audubon, famed naturalist, recorded a flock flying at sixty miles an hour that passed overhead continuously for three entire days, and upon finding their roost he found the ground covered in two inches of bird droppings.

The largest recorded nesting was in Wisconsin in 1871. A conservative estimate of the nesting area was 850 square miles, and estimates put the number of nesting pigeons at 136 million. With as many as 100 nests in a tree, the weight sometimes caused branches to fall off and trees to collapse.

So, what happened? In the late 1800s pigeon hunters followed flocks around the country via rail, searching for nesting grounds. The put their bounty in barrels and then refrigerated box cars and shipped them east. Squab was a tasty delicacy. Operating on an enormous scale, hunters crammed tens of thousands of birds into boxcars. Hunting of passenger pigeons decreased their numbers, especially since they laid only one egg a year.

All this coincided with an explosion in logging, which began destroying the habitat of pigeons just as hunters were destroying the pigeons themselves.

Deforestation of the land played a huge part in their extinction. The birds fed voraciously from the tree nuts of mature beech and oak forests. A Detroit newspaper in the late nineteenth century described the squabs as having "the digestive capacity of half a dozen 14-year-old boys." Once the forests were cut down, the food source disappeared.

In their wake, passenger pigeons left behind stripped fields and ravaged woods; Their droppings, which coated branches and lay a foot thick on the ground, like snow, proved toxic to the undergrowth and fatal to the trees.

The abundance was misleading. In 1900, a boy in Ohio shot a passenger pigeon out of a tree with a twelve-gauge shotgun, killing what was probably the last wild member of the species. A small captive population remained at the Cincinnati Zoo, including a pair named George and Martha. By 1910, Martha was the sole survivor. Officials offered a thousand-dollar reward for a mate, but on September 1, 1914, the last passenger pigeon in the world died.

The last live bird seen in Sheboygan County, as noted in a diary entry, was in the town of Mitchell in the 1880s. A January 3, 1930 Sheboygan Press article noted that the Smithsonian was home to thirty-five to forty stuffed passenger pigeons including Martha. A Milwaukee Sentinel article from February 2, 1933 reported that the Milwaukee Public Museum owned just one pair. In 1963, a Sheboygan Press article highlighted the pair of pigeons on display at the Sheboygan County Museum. They had come from the Carl Benninghaus collection, but because of safety concerns from arsenic used during the taxidermy process, they were removed from the collection in the 1990s and sent to a facility more able to deal with such issues.

Excessive hunting, loss of habitat and overpopulation of the birds themselves created a perfect storm which ended a species. All that remains of the once abundant birds in Wisconsin is a monument in Wyalusing State Park on the Mississippi River.

A rail car and hunters with their catch on a North Dakota pigeon hunt in 1890s.

A group of captive Passenger Pigeons in 1896. This is just a part of a group of pigeons that lived in captivity in the aviary of Professor C.O. Whitman, professor of Zoology at the University of Chicago.

The Wisconsin Historical marker at Wyalusing State Park commemorating the Passenger Pigeon.

Skilled Town of Scott Cabinetmaker Donates Table, a Mosaic Work, to Lincoln Family

What do President Lincoln, Beechwood and the wood-working craft of marquetry have in common? The answer is Peter Glass, an early pioneer and talented artisan.

Peter Glass emigrated from Bavaria to the United States in 1844 and paid his rent by working in a piano factory. But, his passion was making elaborate marquetry furniture. Among the most difficult of wood-working techniques, marquetry is the art of creating pictures in wood by covering whole surfaces with a thin veneer composed of many pieces of wood, like a jigsaw puzzle. His first marquetry table was finished in 1850 and sold to the mayor of Worcester, Massachusetts for $75 ($2400.00 today).

By 1857 Glass had moved his growing family to a farm just north of Beechwood in the town of Scott in Sheboygan County, Wisconsin. Farming fed his family, woodworking was his avocation.

In 1864, Glass spent six months designing and creating a large, tilt-top center table. The following description of the table is given by a Chicago newspaper of 1865: "The table is composed of 20,000 pieces of wood—holly, ebony and black walnut, the last wood being taken from some of the rails split by Mr. Lincoln. The holly is stained in 21 shades. These are wrought in the most exquisite manner into birds, flowers and portraits. There are 17 different kinds of birds, beautiful wreaths, roses, etc. There are portraits of President Lincoln, President Johnson, Lt. General Grant and General Butler."

Glass displayed this piece and its companion worktable in the spring of 1865 in Milwaukee and Chicago for 25 cents in order to fund the transport of the pieces to Washington D.C where he planned to present them to the Lincolns. Unfortunately the tables were still on exhibition in Chicago when Lincoln was assassinated. A few months later Glass gave the tables to the Lincoln family and received a letter of acceptance and thanks from Robert Todd Lincoln.

Glass's craftsmanship is best illustrated in a story from John Gill, a one-time neighbor of Glass, in a letter to Katherine Piper of Plymouth. Gill wrote: "It was sometime in the 1860s that these tables were made. Glass gave one to President Lincoln as a present and took one (or more) to the World's Fair in Paris. There, someone told Glass that his table was painted. Glass grabbed a wood plane, and before anyone could stop him, ran the plane halfway across the table. It was easy to see it was not painted."

One of Glass's inlaid tables had as many as 96,320 pieces of wood and was sold for $1400. The table was constructed after the Lincoln table and also taken to the 1867 Paris Exposition. Unable to sell it, Glass brought it back to the United States and raffled it for $2,000 in 1872.

Along with the mosaic tables, Glass is also known to have earlier carved St. Michael Catholic Church's ornate altars in the town of Mitchell. A superb example of old world craftsmanship, the altars was ornately carved and rich in intricate design. Along with the main altar were two side altars, one with the Virgin Mary and the baby Jesus, and the other with Jesus as an adult. The altar railings were also done by Glass. These works of art were removed from the sanctuary of St. Michael in the early 1960s when the church was thought to be in need of an update. The altar rail was removed at the same time.

Glass worked on his art until three years prior to his death in 1901. After he died, his family scattered to all parts of the United States, many owning pieces of his life's work. And more than 100 years after his burial in St. Michael's cemetery people still discuss and celebrate his career and his achievements.

Not a bad legacy!

Peter Glass, marquetry master, is seen here with one of his designs, the Mary Todd Lincoln table, circa 1865.

In 2003, the Milwaukee Art Museum scheduled an exhibit in its Decorative Arts Gallery entitled "Skin Deep: Three Masters of American Inlaid Furniture." Peter Glass was one of the three masters honored.

Above: St. Michael Catholic Church, town of Mitchell circa 1880. The original altars were designed and carved by Peter Glass.

Break Out the Golf Clubs, Spring is Here

The game of golf was born on the windswept terrain of eastern Scotland, and evolved gradually into the game we know today. Golf made the leap across the Atlantic in 1743 when there is record of the sale of 96 golf clubs and 432 golf balls to a Mr. Deas in Charleston, South Carolina. It took until 1888 for the first permanent golf club, appropriately named St. Andrew's, to be established in Yonkers, New York.

The first golf played in Sheboygan County was near Lake View Park on Sheboygan's south side in 1899, but that temporary course was plowed under in favor of a crop of potatoes. Apparently the farmer who owned the land didn't appreciate this new sport.

In May of 1905, the Sheboygan Country Club was organized. The club leased seventeen acres adjacent to the old insane asylum and poor farm, west and south of today's Vollrath Company, and created the county's first nine-hole course. This proximity to the hospital occasionally led to humorous encounters. Golfer Herman Roenitz recalled that as he walked down the edge of a fairway one day, an inmate of the asylum called to him in a high-pitched voice saying, "You think we're crazy, but you're the one chasing a little white ball."

By 1928, however, the directors of the club knew they needed an 18-hole course to keep up with changing times and ever increasing demand for quality courses. The club purchased 161 acres along the Pigeon River west of the city for such a course. The final price tag for the course was near $130,000.00 ($1,751,235.26 today).

A Gala Grand Opening, for the newly named Pine Hills, was held in May of 1930. Edward Hammett's moniker was chosen from eighty-six entries in a naming contest for the new Sheboygan Country Club. Pine Hills is really an a.k.a. as the name was never legally changed from the Sheboygan Country Club.

Quit Qui Oc Golf Club in Elkhart Lake was Sheboygan County's second golf course. The land purchased for the club was the seventy-four acre Edward Wolf farm located on the south side of Elkhart Lake. The first play on the course was July 1, 1923 according to the Sheboygan Press Telegram. The original 18-hole layout opened in 1927, but during World War II the back nine was abandoned due to lack of play.

Unique among golf clubs of the 1920s, Quit Qui Oc had an observation tower from which play over the entire nine-hole course could be watched. The round tower-like structure was made from the old farm silo.

At one time fifty caddies, managed by a Caddy Master, were available for golfers, but they were eventually replaced by golf carts. One of the earliest carts was perfected by Quit Qui Oc's very own golf pro, Ed Leverenz, in the early 1950s. "Birdie" was powered by a five-horse gas motor and could travel from 2 to 5 mph depending on the terrain.

William Harder made history in August of 1926 when his round ended unexpectedly. Stuck in a sand hazard on the fifth hole of Quit Qui Oc, his round of golf was interrupted when, as The Sheboygan Press reported, "Sheriff Jack Case and the even more hefty form of Undersheriff Hugo Fesing suddenly appeared in a line between the ball and the green on Hole No. 5." Harder was wanted for forging checks in Lombard, Illinois, writing bad checks in Elkhart Lake and Wisconsin Dells, and also for taking a mortgaged car out of state (Illinois). Humorously, it was editorialized that Harder showed very poor form on his swing, noting his golf stick sent up a cloud of sand as he was read the charges.

Owned by the Wiese family since 1955, Quit Qui Oc added a third nine holes about ten years ago.

Sheboygan County is home to nearly a dozen beautiful golf courses ranging from Sunset Hills in Sheboygan Falls, a par three course, to the every challenging links course at Whistling Straits.

Sheboygan Country Club's first clubhouse

Quit Qui Oc's clubhouse is seen above. Ernest Killick, experienced golf pro of the Fort Meyers Yacht and Golf club in Florida, was secured as the Quit Qui Oc pro for the summer months. Mr. Killick was an experienced instructor and club maker. His father learned the profession at Brighton, England. Beautiful green pasture land provided fairways which were deemed top-notch.

The observation tower, fashioned from an old silo, was a novelty at QQO golf course in Elkhart Lake.

Above: Lake Street in Elkhart Lake looking east toward the golf course. Future fun spot at left. Image taken circa 1900. Sheboygan Press-Telegram– Friday, May 16, 1924– *Elkhart Lake's New Golf Course One of the Finest in Wisconsin.* The great American game which we stole from the hardy Scotch has for years had a fine standing among the patrons of Pine Point summer resort, Elkhart Lake. This great resort, one of the largest in the entire northwest has long been a popular outing place. Residents of all of Elkhart's resorts made up the elite membership list of the private club.

A nine-hole extension of Quit Qui Oc was dedicated on August 23, 1928 and there was an exhibition match between Francis Gallet, professional at Milwaukee, and Billy Sixty, golf and sports editor of the Milwaukee Journal. The addition made this one of the best eighteen hole courses in this part of America.

Women were an important part of QQO golf club from the outset. This image was taken in the 1920s.

More information about the earliest golf in the county.

The Sheboygan Country Club represents the history of golfing in Sheboygan County. The first golf played here was at Lake View in 1899 by John Homiller and Herman Roenitz according to Roenitz who related the story at the dedication of Pine Hills Country Club in 1930.

On May 24, 1905, the first real golf club, the Sheboygan Country Club, was organized with Watson Crocker as president. The golfers leased the old Lyman farm and in 1906 moved a cottage from Lake View to serve as a club house. (The Lyman farm was just west and south of the intersection of Wilgus Road and Kohler Memorial Drive.)

By 1914 the clubhouse had become inadequate and an addition was built. A grand opening of the clubhouse and an extended ninehole golf course was held in June 1915. The country club comprised 48 acres of rolling land almost completely encircled by trees-orchards to the north and a pine grove to the south.

The remodeled clubhouse, a one and one half story frame L-shaped structure, contained a reception room with fireplace, dining room, kitchen, ballroom, sunroom, ladies lounge and locker room. The men's quarters were contained in a two story frame house located northwest of the clubhouse

The furnishings of the house were all manufactured in the county - the American Mfg. Co., Acker Electrical Co. and the Kohler Co.

In addition to golf, there was also a small ball diamond, two double tennis courts, a basketball court and play area for small children with slides, swings and sand boxes.

The entrance to the country club was marked by two pillars surmounted with urns. A cinder drive ran from the waiting station of the interurban car sheds in the rear..

All of the buildings were painted grey with white trim and had red roofs.

In 1925 members of the Sheboygan Country Club held a meeting to consider plans for enlarging the clubhouse. The committee recommendation was voted down by the members. By 1928, however, the directors of the club were looking into the establishment of an 18-hole course and the membership voted to take the necessary steps to make the proposed course a reality. Work began in August 1928 on land located north of the Howards Road west of the point where Wilgus Road intersects and a mile from the city limits. The Sheboygan Country Club invested $125,000 in the new course and clubhouse. Harry B. Smead, Chicago landscape architect, was the general contractor for the laying of the course.

Thirty-one Years and a Lifetime Ago
The End of H.C. Prange Co.

As Sheboygan city leaders announce an agreement to purchase the former Prange's (Boston Store) property at Eighth and Wisconsin Streets, and start a new phase in the property's history, it's fitting to remember the demise of Prange's which changed the face of retail business in downtown Sheboygan thirty-one years ago this week.

H.C. Prange Company, Sheboygan's biggest department store, was evacuated at mid-morning on May 4, 1983 after a break in a 6-inch underground water main about the size of a fifty cent piece, was noticed about 9 a.m.

The water main rupture, powered by city pressure, undermined ground under the basement floor, causing support pillars around the building's escalator system to shift and the upper floors to sag.

The Sheboygan Fire Department was summoned to the store to pump water from the basement. The floors of poured concrete construction buckled less than an hour after fire fighters arrived, in a 30-foot diameter area around the store's escalator system.

An employee of a local engineering firm, who was inside the building after the incident, said the basement floor dropped 14 to 15 inches near a support column where the water main had broken. Each floor above the support column had correspondingly sagged, he said. Customers in the store at the time said debris fell from the sagging ceilings as they were fleeing. Driverless shopping carts rolled to the middle of the store, crystal and glass slid off their shelves as floors sagged.

Customers and employees were outwardly calm, but walking the sloped floors toward the escalators, caused anxiety. Shoppers were afraid that the floors would collapse. Mannequins sprawled on the floor, looking like dead people, clothes and arms askew.

About fifty people made their way down the escalators. Elderly women evacuated from the fourth floor beauty salon area with their hair in rollers and with towels around their shoulders. Many had their hair finished in the parking lot with stylists working from their car trunks.

In leaving the building as quickly as they did, employees left personal effects behind. Merchandise on order for customers also remained in the store. Causing the most anxiety were the bridal dresses needed for May and June weddings.

The incident resulted in no injuries, but forced the closing of the store. Initially it was thought the store would be back in business in a couple of days, but after inspection it was found that damage was catastrophic. A new store would be built. Demolition of the old four story classic was scheduled for fall of 1983.

But, a massive fire broke out on Sunday evening, October 16, 1983. The inferno that started about 7:30pm, filled the night sky and intensified as winds gusted to 25 miles per hour. Raging for more than two hours, it could be seen from fifteen miles away. Neighbors were encouraged to soak their roofs with hoses to prevent further fires.

The focus of the fire fight was to prevent the spread of the fire to the City Hall annex (old Mead Library), St. Clement's Church and school and the Kohler Arts Center. Major damage was done to the gym at St. Clement's where the roof was completely burned through and the floor extensively damaged from water.

The Prange store was in the process of being torn down by Buteyn Excavating and Grading and should have been completed within a week or two, after which construction on the new store was to have begun. Arson was suspected.

The old Prange's was no more. Other companies have closed their doors, but Prange's was the heart and soul of the downtown. Sheboygan weathered the loss, but the memories still linger

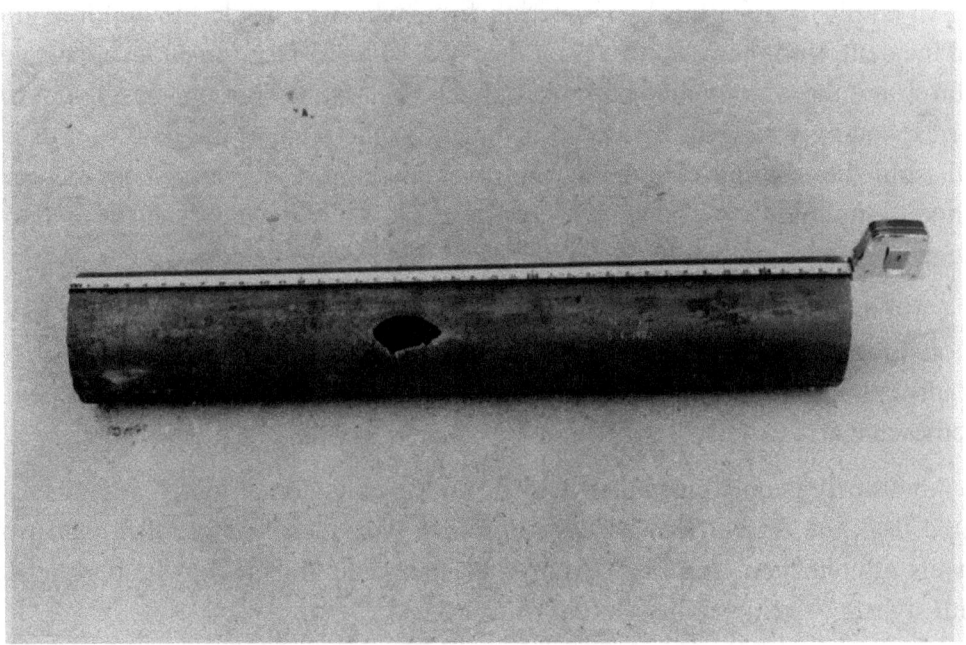

The six inch underground pipe with hole, the size of a quarter, that leaked causing the catastrophic damage to H. C. Prange Store in May, 1983.

Above: H.C. Prange escalator damaged in floor collapse, third floor south location.

Below: Aftermath of the H.C. Prange fire as fire still smolders.

Sheboygan Observes V-E Day – May 8, 1945

A V-E Day celebration like no other took place in London. American sailors and laughing girls formed a conga line down the middle of Piccadilly. A crowd of more than 50,000 Londoners reveled in Whitehall. Bands played, flags flew and the air was filled with fireworks. At Buckingham Palace, Prime Minister Winston Churchill appeared with the Royal Family on a balcony overlooking a pondered jubilant crowd that packed the square below. Great Britain's long nightmare was nearly over.

But it was a far different story in Sheboygan County. " Prayerfully, hopefully, Sheboygan County residents observed V-E Day" reported the Sheboygan Press on that historic Tuesday morning in May of 1945. There was restrained excitement as county residents pondered the events of the previous days.

On April 30, as Russian troops fought to within yards of his subterranean bunker, Adolph Hitler ended his life. Hitler was unaware that the German surrender had already begun. The Italians had surrendered long ago. Only the Japanese were left.

So, it was no surprise when German General Jodl surrendered unconditionally to Allied Commander Eisenhower on May 7, in the French city of Reims. After six terrible years, the war in Europe was over. Thirty-two and a half million men, women, and children were dead, 226 of them from Sheboygan County alone.

Even with President Truman's radio confirmation that morning, Sheboygan experienced no great outburst of emotion. No peeling church bells, no shrieking factory whistles, no joyous hysteria greeted the news.

Locally, retail stores closed their doors until 1 p.m. The county courthouse and city hall offices suspended work for the day. Parochial and public school held special programs and were then dismissed for the morning.

Taverns closed for 24-hours to prevent a victory celebration fueled more by alcohol than by patriotism. Only two 'chiselers' remained open. Radloff's Tavern, 2333 North 15th Street and Babisch's Tavern, 1442 South 12th Street were fined and castigated for the offense.

Although, mainly calm, a former Sheboyganite related that at least one fight broke out when some unthinking dolt expressed the fact that he was sorry to see the war end because overtime, too, would end. The foolish man was promptly encouraged to change his opinion.

But, Sheboygan's celebration was tempered with the grim truth that although Europe, bathed in blood for more than five years, was free, on the other side of the world Japan was still on the march. The full task was only half achieved. And America was fully involved.

Sheboygan's citizens held a civic observance at the Armory that Tuesday, May 8, 1945. Stirring music was provided by Wuerl's Band. The choirs of Central and North high schools sang patriotic numbers with fervor.

Carol Hagedorn, a Central High School student, solemnly read a list of 44 gold-star servicemen, all 44 of them former Central students. The student body stood with bowed heads during the reading. The audience joined the school's A Cappella choir in the singing of "This Is My Country" and "America the Beautiful."

President Harry Truman, who turned 61 that day, dedicated the victory to the memory of his predecessor, Franklin D. Roosevelt, who had died of a stroke less than a month before. The country was still officially in mourning, with flags flying at half-mast for the full thirty days.

One small measure of celebration showed in the lighting of Statue of Liberty and the dome of the Capitol building in Washington D.C. They were illuminated that night for the first time since December 1941.

It would be another three months before the war would end, and another year until every soldier would return home. But, on May 8, 1945, as Sheboygan quietly gave thanks, the end was in sight.

Stars and Stripes Headline – Tuesday, May 8, 1945 Victory, Nazis Reveal Surrender to Western Allies, Russia. Stars and Stripes is the American newspaper for the military.

Above: Sheboygan Press Headline- Monday, May 7, 1945 Germany Surrenders.
Below: London Celebration in Piccadilly Circus.

Harry Selfridge and his Wisconsin Connections

Tomorrow night (May 18, 2014) PBS airs the final episode of this season's popular Masterpiece series, Mr. Selfridge. The back story of this series has one great connection to Wisconsin and one to Sheboygan County.

A flamboyant entrepreneur and showman, Harry Gordon Selfridge sought to provide shoppers with the ultimate spending experience. Much of the consumer culture that surrounds us today began in the mind of this ambitious boy from Wisconsin.

Selfridge was born in 1858 in Ripon, Wisconsin. His father, Robert, left the Fond du Lac County town in 1861 to serve in the Civil War and failed to return home. Harry never saw his father again. Soon after Lois Selfridge moved the family to Jackson, Michigan to be nearer her family.

In 1875, Harry left for Chicago where he went to work for Marshall Field as a stock boy. But, that didn't last long. He soon moved to the advertising department where he employed phrases such as "the customer is always right" and "give the lady what she wants". Nicknamed 'Mile-A-Minute-Harry', Selfridge made sweeping changes capitalizing on the huge advances in new technology. He installed dozens of phones; increased the lighting and even lit the beautiful window displays at night – a first for a Chicago store.

As a result of the innovations at Marshal Field's flagship store on State Street he made partner at age 29.

In 1906, after vacationing in England and ready for a change, he decided to in build his own department store in Oxford Street, London. The new store, Selfridge's, opened to the public on March 15, 1909 and was a marvel: nine Otis elevators; a state-of-the-art sprinkler system; five impressive floors and a roof terrace with a garden. More than 100 departments sold everything from swimsuits to sable coats.

Few from the Ripon area realize that their hometown boy is credited with creating two of retail's most popular phrases: "Only__ more shopping days 'til Christmas!" and "The customer is always right."

The local connection with the Selfridge story involves actor Jeremy Piven who portrays Harry Selfridge in the Masterpiece series. Piven grew up in Evanston, Illinois, but spent his teenage summers at Camp Harand in Elkhart Lake.

An article in the March 17, 1955 Sheboygan Press states, "Historic Osthoff's

Resort at Elkhart Lake has been purchased by Chicago residents who will convert it into a Camp of Theatre Arts. The property which includes 60 acres, 19 buildings and 500 feet of lake frontage was purchased by Sulie and Pearl Harand. The new owners conduct the Studio of Theatre Arts in Chicago. They plan to have the camp open from June 27 to August 21 and will specialize in drama, song interpretation and ballet along with normal camp life."

Another Press article from May 25, 1966 boasted of Harand's graduates and patrons. Among them were Shelley Berman, Tom Bosley and Forest Tucker of F Troop fame.

Campers were divided into groups designated by names of shows and were known as "Haranders." In the 1960s, Camp Harand hosted up to 375 campers during the summer season. The curriculum focused on musical theater with an emphasis on community spirit and equal opportunity. The studio was also the first to combine training in all three musical theater disciplines- singing, dancing, and acting.

A Harand camper in the 1980s, Jeremy Piven once asked, "how many places in the world can you go to as a kid and get fulfillment performing in plays without all the politics—and still get to play sports all day long?" He described Camp Harand as the ultimate fantasy camp, one with sports and acting together.

In 1989, the Harand family sold the camp property in Elkhart Lake and moved to Wayland Academy in Beaver Dam. In 2005, the camp relocated to Carthage College in Kenosha.

Sulie and Pearl Harand took an innovative approach to the arts. They built a non-competitive environment, where everyone could share parts in a show and no one was a star. Everyone was there to develop self-confidence and improve communication skills. Add to that, sports and the activities of camp life, and you had a winning combination, right here in Elkhart Lake.

So, in the words of Paul Harvey, "That's the rest of the story."

Harry Selfridge, 1858-1947

Selfridge's Department Store. Founded by American business man Henry Gordon Selfridge, Oxford Street's most famous department store opened in 1909 and is the second largest store in London after Harrods. During the 1920s and 1930s the store's roof hosted a terraced garden, cafes and an all-girl gun club. The store was bombed 3 times during WWII causing extensive damage to the roof garden. The large display windows were bricked up as a safety precaution. Camp Harand, seen below, was located right on the shore of Elkhart Lake.

Sheboygan Calmly Greeted Halley's Comet

In the spring of 1910 the Dalai Lama fled Tibet to escape the Chinese, President Taft began the tradition of throwing out the first ball on baseball's opening day, King Edward VII of Great Britain died and Montana's Glacier National Park was formed. In May of 1910 the citizens of Sheboygan County also braced themselves for a close encounter with Halley's Comet.

Halley's Comet is a periodic comet last seen here in 1986 and expected to return in 2061. Named after Edmond Halley, an Oxford mathematician who observed that it came every seventy-six years on the anniversary of significant world events, it was especially significant to Christians who believed it to be the Star of Bethlehem that guided the Wise Men.

The comet is visible for slightly less than three months each occurrence. The earliest known written record of the comet is by the Chinese in 240 BC.

Mark Twain, author and humorist, born in 1835 as the comet approached, said in 1910, "I came in with Halley's Comet... It is coming again ... and I expect to go out with it... The Almighty has said, no doubt: 'Now here are these two unaccountable freaks; they came in together, they must go out together." Sure enough, he died on April 21, 1910, the first day the comet was visible.

Celestial phenomena have triggered apocalyptic hysteria many times throughout history. The comet of 79 A.D. was blamed for the eruption of Vesuvius that led to the destruction of the cities of Pompeii and Herculaneum. Its appearance in 1665 was said to have caused the Black Plague that killed tens of thousands in London. In 1835 it was blamed for several things, including the fall of the Alamo and a fire in New York City that raged for nearly a week.

In 1910, when astronomers from Wisconsin's very own Yerkes Observatory announced that the planet would pass through the tail of Halley's Comet in May of that year alarmists and tabloids spread the erroneous rumor that poisonous gas within the comet would spell doom for the world's population. They warned Cyanogen gas in the comet's tail would "snuff out" all life. Shysters capitalized on the resulting fear, selling "comet pills" and "anti-comet umbrellas" that would counteract any lethal effects.

During the night of May 18, 1910, when the Earth passed through the tail of Halley's, some people took precautions by sealing the chimneys, windows, and doors of their houses. Others confessed to crimes they had committed because they did not expect to survive the night, and a few panic-stricken people actually committed suicide. Church services were held for overflow crowds, and people in the countryside took to their storm shelters.

But, by 1910 people were also divided in their thinking. Along with the fearful, there were skeptics who turned the event into festivity. A strangely frivolous mood in cities caused thousands of people to gather in restaurants, coffee houses, parks, and on the rooftops of apartment buildings to await their imaginary doom in the company of friends.

Locally, Miss Emmeline Cole stated in a Sheboygan Telegram article, "The year 1910 is that of the reappearance of Halley's Comet. The best proof that people are less superstitious now than they were in the past was shown by the fact that there were few people of any one's acquaintance who showed great fear that the near approach of the heavenly wanderer. While there were a few persons comparatively whose fear led them to commit self-destruction; the large body of the people awaited the predicted collision with the comet with a philosophical calmness that did them great credit. The people of Sheboygan County did not show that they were in the least disturbed."

The Sheboygan Historical Review of July 1910 reported, "Late in the afternoon of May 18, 1910 the earth was scheduled to enter the tail of Halley's Comet. If the wanderer came in contact with the earth or the atmosphere there was nothing unusual to indicate it."

It seems the residents of Sheboygan County were sufficiently educated and streetwise to avoid falling for the purveyors of snake oil found everywhere at the time. By the end of the summer of 1910 news coverage of the event disappeared. The world went on and so did the Comet; there were more important events to report. Looking back it seems slightly reminiscent of Y2K doesn't it?

At left: A photo of Halley's Comet, still in sight on May 4, 1910, thirteen days after Mark Twain's death.

An ad for Hope's Anti-Comet pills guaranteed to be an elixir for escaping the wrath of the heavens.

Yerke's Observatory, seen here in 1892, is operated by the University of Chicago and located in Williams' Bay, Wisconsin near Lake Geneva. It has the world's largest refracting telescope used in scientific research.

Edmond Halley was an English astronomer, geophysicist, mathematician, meteorologist, and physicist who is best known for computing the orbit of the comet named for him, Halley's Comet.

Plank Road Surveyor Paine Helped Build Brooklyn Bridge

The Brooklyn Bridge stands out among engineering wonders of the 19th Century, and when it opened on May 24, 1883 it spanned the East River connecting the cities of New York and Brooklyn. The bridge, with its imposing stone towers and graceful steel cables, took fourteen years to build and cost $15 million (more than $320 million today). At least two dozen people died in the process, including its architect.

John Roebling, the Brooklyn Bridge's creator, was a great pioneer in the design of steel suspension bridges. But, just before construction began in 1869, Roebling was critically injured while taking a few final compass readings across the East River. A boat smashed the toes on one of his feet, and three weeks later he died of tetanus. His son, Washington Roebling, took over as chief engineer.

To achieve a solid foundation for the bridge, workers excavated the riverbed in massive wooden boxes called caissons. These airtight chambers were secured to the river's floor by enormous granite blocks; pressurized air was pumped in to keep water and debris out.

The hot, dense air in the caissons gave workers blinding headaches, itchy skin, bloody noses and slowed heartbeats—but they were relatively safe. The journey to and from the depths of the East River, however, could be deadly. To get down into the caissons, the workers rode in small iron containers called airlocks. As the airlock descended into the river, it filled with compressed air. This air made it possible to breathe in the caisson and kept the water from seeping in, but it also dissolved a dangerous amount of gas into the workers' bloodstreams. When the workers resurfaced, the dissolved gases in their blood were quickly released.

This often caused a plethora of painful symptoms known as "caisson disease" or "the bends": excruciating joint pain, paralysis, convulsions and, in some cases, death. More than 100 workers suffered from the disease, including Washington Roebling himself, who remained partially paralyzed for the rest of his life.

Now, you ask, what does the Brooklyn Bridge have to do with Sheboygan County? The connection comes with surveyor, William Paine. Born in Chester, New Hampshire, Paine moved to Sheboygan County in 1848 with his parents and worked as the Sheboygan County Surveyor for more than ten years beginning about 1850. An active surveyor, he filed 174 surveys during his tenure laying the Sheboygan-Fond du Lac Plank Road for construction. He also laid out sections of road west of Plymouth through the "potash kettles".

Paine had a gift for measuring and invention. On July 10, 1860, he received a patent for a steel measuring tape. In a time when all other surveyors were dragging heavy chains, or ropes, or worse, through the brush to measure distances, Paine was using a modern steel measuring tape, and was even correcting his measurements to allow for the thermal expansion and contraction of the steel tape. Some reports claim that the development of the material that was used for the hoops in women's hoop skirts made the steel tape possible.

In 1861, at the beginning of the Civil War, Paine enlisted in the Fourth Wisconsin Regiment. His skill as a surveyor got him work as a topographic engineer or map maker for the Union Army. Paine worked mainly under General Meade, Commander of the Army of the Potomac. Soft-spoken and unassuming, William Paine was without fear. In 1863, wearing civilian clothes, Paine snuck through Confederate lines, and mapped the route from Washington D.C. to Richmond. He was also at Appomattox Courthouse on the day of Lee's surrender to Grant.

In April 1869, Paine became assistant engineer on the Brooklyn Bridge project, working under Chief Engineer John Roebling.

While working on the bridge he invented several gadgets. One was a communication device, which allowed people located on the outside, to give directions to those working below the river in the caissons. He also invented an instrument to test the strength of the wire which was used in the suspension cables.

As the bridge neared completion, William Paine was made responsible for the design and construction of the cable railroad which would run on the bridge.

Paine died of heart disease in Cleveland in 1890. At the time of his death, he was described in the New York Times, as "one of the foremost engineers of the country". His prized measuring tapes remained available into the 1920s. It turned out to be quite a career for a simple surveyor who cut his teeth in the wilds of Sheboygan County.

William Paine, surveyor, worked early on in his career mapping out Sheboygan County. He later used his skills during the Civil War and then helped build the Brooklyn Bridge.

The Brooklyn Bridge is a bridge in New York City and is one of the oldest suspension bridges in the United States. Completed in 1883, it connects the boroughs of Manhattan and Brooklyn by spanning the East River.

Civil War surveyors seen at Camp Winfield Scott, near Yorktown, Virginia, May 2, 1862. Capt. Paine is the seated man without a hat. Standing second from the right is Allen Pinkerton. The rest are all believed to be U.S. Coast Survey civilians. The man furthest to the right in the photograph has one of Paine's tapes hanging at his hip.

By 1902, when the Brooklyn Bridge was fully operational, it accommodated horses, horse-drawn trolleys, trains and pedestrians, and they were — all of them — charged a toll: one cent for pedestrians, two cents for livestock and 20 if you had a carriage pulled by horses. More than 340,000 people crossed daily that year. By 1907, the bridge's peak year, 426,000 people crossed every day. The toll was abolished in 1911.

John Roebling

Star Dusk Drive-In provided 35 years of memories

A new chapter in motion picture history started on June 6, 1933; the first-ever park-in theater opened to a packed house in Camden, New Jersey. Admission was 25 cents per car and 25 cents per person. Movie goers were treated to the British comedy Wives Beware.

The "drive-in" theater, a term not used until later, was the creation of Richard Hollingshead. Inspired by his generously-sized mother's struggle to sit comfortably in theater seats he came up with the idea of an open-air cinema where customers watched movies in the comfort of their own cars. He experimented in the driveway of his own house with different projection and sound equipment, mounting a 1928 Kodak projector on the hood of his car, pinning a screen to some trees, and placing a radio behind the screen for sound.

In 1948, there were just 3 outdoor theaters in Wisconsin, but by 1954 they peaked with sixty-four open air venues. The outdoor fad soon after began a slow decline until the 1980s when numbers dropped precipitously. Today there are just nine remaining in Wisconsin.

Remember the Highway 57 Outdoor Theatre in Cedarburg, the Lake Park Outdoor in Fond du Lac and the Lake Vue Outdoor in Manitowoc. All are gone today.

Sheboygan's very own Star Dusk Theater (not Star Dust) opened in June 1949. Located on fifteen acres on the northeast corner of South 12th Street and County EE on the city's south side, the business was built by Sheldon Grengs and Claude Wardian for an investment of about $80,000. It could accommodate 600 cars and had eleven ramps to elevate their front ends for better viewing.

The 'mammoth' screen was about 50 x 40 feet in size and covered in reflective paint for an improved picture. The very large screen tower was bright yellow with the name of the drive-in spelled out in bold red letters. The entire venue was constructed by Quasius Construction in just over six weeks.

By 1955 the screen had been enlarged to more than eight stories, 80 x 50 feet in size. "Buck Nights" were held every Thursday and Friday where one dollar paid for a carload. Shows changed three times a week and double features were shown on Saturdays and Sundays. Cartoon features were added and everything was shown in "vivid technicolor". Every car had an in-car speaker which occasionally left the theater still stuck in some embarrassed driver's window.

A full page ad for the grand opening advertised a whole range of benefits: You may smoke if you like; What a break for us old folks. Now we can go to the movies, too; If there's room for Fido in your car, he's welcome, too; We baby your baby, free bottle warmers at the snack bar.

Theater management was committed to the success of the grand opening of the Star Dusk. Free admission was offered for the first day. Ads boasted two 'swell' features, Just For You with Bing Crosby and Jane Wyman; and Caribbean with John Payne and Arlene Dahl. Each car attending was also given a certificate for two free gallons of gas.

The drive-in theater was a family favorite because the entire family and a couple of friends could pile into the car in pajamas with popcorn and Kool-Aid and have a great time for as little as a dollar.

Interestingly, the Wesley Methodist Church of Sheboygan held drive-in church services at the Star Dusk on Sundays during the summer of 1955. The pulpit, organ and altar were stationed on the roof of the refreshment stand and coffee and doughnuts were served to parishioners to give them strength in their worship. The church hoped to reach those driving through the county on those Sunday mornings.

The Star Dusk Drive-In closed on September 3, 1984. No more steamed up car windows or sneaking in in the trunk of the Buick. No more mosquito swarms coming in open windows. It was the end of an era. The screen and outbuildings were torn down a decade later. The site is now home to a mobile home park.

Peaking in the late 1950s, there were almost 5000 drive-ins. Today, there are only 366 operating in the United States. The rise of television and VHS, and more importantly, increased land prices, led to the genre's downfall.

Today the few remaining theaters are struggling to make the change to digital format. Costs range from $70,000 to $100,000 per theater, far too much for most small businesses. Research done by the Los Angeles Times estimated that only 10% of the remaining drive-ins made the change as of 2013. But happily, some communities are stepping up and choosing to help with conversion costs just to preserve a part of their history. Here, in Sheboygan County, we may not have an outdoor theater, but we have great memories.

This is an ad for the first Outdoor Theater in New Jersey

This Outdoor Theater image reminds us of a cozy Friday night in front of the big screen.

This view of the Star Dusk site in Sheboygan shows the concession stand and ramps for better viewing in June 1949. The site is still under construction.

This image is of early construction at the Star Dusk Outdoor Theater in Sheboygan, Quasius Construction Company built the screen, etc.

The concession stand at the Star Dusk Theater in Sheboygan in June of 1949, Sheboygan Press photo.

The Golden Arches Arrived in 1958

Friday, June 19, 1958 brought the grand opening of Sheboygan County's very first McDonald's. George Tuttle, the local owner-manager of this pioneer McDonald's, built his "hamburger palace" on North Avenue just west of Calumet Drive in the city of Sheboygan.

The drive-in and walk-up, fast-food restaurant was the 121st McDonald's franchise granted in the United States and the third in Wisconsin. It offered only three food items that year: hamburgers with the works for fifteen cents, French fries for ten cents and cheeseburgers, also with the works, for twenty cents. Beverages on the menu included triple thick shakes, soda and coffee. No special orders for the first few years! And no tipping, a bonus for our ever-frugal local residents.

A family of five could eat for $2.25 and enjoy America's favorite hamburger. The advertisement boasted "No dishes to wash. No mess to clean." The restaurant was also open on Sundays, something not commonly seen in the 1960s because of Blue Laws.

This dining brainchild took off when Richard and Maurice McDonald changed their successful California drive-in to a more streamlined system with a simple menu of just hamburgers, cheeseburgers, French fries, shakes, soft drinks, and apple pie. Carhops were eliminated to make McDonald's a self-service operation. The brothers took great care in setting up their kitchen like an assembly line to ensure maximum efficiency. This new "McDonald's" opened on December 12, 1948.

The McDonald brothers crafted the golden arches outside of their building to look like a big "M" in 1952.

In 1954, Ray Kroc, a seller of Multimixer milkshake machines, learned that the McDonald brothers were using eight of his machines in their San Bernardino restaurant. His curiosity was piqued, and he went to take a look at their restaurant.

Believing the McDonalds' formula was sure to succeed, Kroc dreamed of franchises throughout the country. The brothers were skeptical, but Kroc offered to take the reins and the risk for setting up the new stores. A partnership was formed. Kroc's first restaurant opened on April 15, 1955 in Des Plaines, Illinois, but he eventually bought out the brothers.

By 1961 the "Golden Arches" became part of Ray Kroc's iconic McDonald's logo.

In the 1960s, McDonald's sought a menu item that would tackle the dilemma of lagging Friday sales. Back then, most American Catholics abstained from meat on Fridays throughout the year as a form of penance. As a result, McDonald's was losing Friday customers to competitors like Big Boy, which served a fish sandwich. To boost Friday sales and cater to Catholics, Ray Kroc hoped to introduce the Hula Burger - grilled pineapple on a bun. But, in a test market run the Filet-o-Fish was the winner, far outpacing the Hula Burger. It was added to the original menu in 1962 and has been a hit ever since.

Perhaps, the most important new item introduced as the company grew was the Big Mac launched in 1967. This popular sandwich consists of, as the immortal jingle put it, "two all-beef patties, special sauce, lettuce, cheese, pickles, onions on a sesame-seed bun", a ditty every kid of the 1960s and 1970s knew by heart.

Fast food in America, was actually a turn of the 20th century concept. First seen in a cafeteria-style Automat in New York City, prepared foods were displayed behind small glass windows with coin operated slots. This launched the idea of "take-out" food. But, White Castle, home of the Slider hamburger, founded in 1921 in Kansas City, is generally considered to be the first "fast food" restaurant in the country.

As of 2013, McDonald's sold in excess of 300 billion hamburgers, and employs 1.8 million people in more than 34,500 restaurants in 119 countries. Sheboygan County now has six of its own, four in Sheboygan, one in the city of Plymouth, and one in Sheboygan Falls.

Love it or hate it, McDonald's will always be something of a cultural icon.

This image shows the original McDonald's Restaurant, owned by Richard and Maurice McDonald in San Bernardino, California, circa 1948. The sign crows, Buy 'Em by the Bag!

Sheboygan's first McDonald's. This is a photo of the Golden Arches located on North Avenue in Sheboygan. It was the first of four McDonalds to eventually be built in Sheboygan. The photo was taken during the 1950s. Remember when it was just a drive-in with no special orders; Before the Big Mac, the McRib and Supersized everything.

The original Kroc McDonald's menu of 1955.

Hamburger 15¢
Cheeseburger 19¢
Triple Thick Shakes 20¢
Golden French Fries 10¢
Soda 10¢
Orange Drink 10¢
Cold Milk 12¢

Grand Opening

TOMORROW ... FRIDAY, JUNE 19

FREE Gifts for everyone

SEE this Wonderful New HAMBURGER PALACE ...

McDonald's

On NORTH AVE. Just West of CALUMET DRIVE

Home of America's Favorite Hamburger

still only 15¢

TRY THE "ALL AMERICAN"

Come in and get acquainted. Try an "All American" at McDonald's ... 100% Pure Beef Hamburger, only 15¢ ... rich, creamy, triple-thick Milk Shakes, only 20¢ ... crisp, delicious French Fries, only 10¢ ... a meal for only 45¢ ... for a family of five ... only $2.25.

a pleasure every family can afford!

Mom ... dad ... and kiddies love it. Load up the car and bring the family ... no dishes to wash ... no mess to clean. You'll get *fast*, cheerful, and courteous service ... plenty of free parking ... no car hops ... no tipping ... just the tastiest food in town ... at extra thrifty prices.

HAMBURGER ... SHAKE ... FRENCH FRIES
McDONALD'S "ALL AMERICAN MEAL" ONLY
45¢ ... FOR A FAMILY OF FIVE $2.25

look for the drive-in with the arches **McDonald's**

Open 11 a.m. to 11 p.m. Daily and Sunday. 11 a.m. to Midnight Friday and Saturday.

We're Happy To Have Had A Part In The Construction Of McDonald's Drive-In

EARL DE SOMBRE ... General Contractor

| **Gehrke Sheet Metal** | **Weinkauf Electric Co.** | **Mark Eggebeen Sons** |
| Sheet Metal Work | Electrical Wiring | Painting and Decorating |

| **Reliance Construction Co.** | **South Side Hardware and Plumbing Co.** |
| Black Topping | Plumbing |

Wisconsin's Beer Bar Phenomenon

Minor bars, teen bars or beer bars, whatever you called them, were part of a thirty-year chapter in Wisconsin life that often brings chuckles from those who lived through that memorable era.

On June 15, 1940 the Magnet on Main Street in Oshkosh became the first tavern in Wisconsin to be issued a beer-only license. It was at the vanguard of what would become a controversial Wisconsin institution, the teenage beer bar where kids 18-20 years old could enjoy a beer usually accompanied by great music and dancing.

Locally, there were many establishments to frequent including: The Patio north of Kohler, Harold's 23 Club in Sheboygan Falls, The Red Bird, Uncle Gus', Max's and The Bitter End in Sheboygan, Oak Park in Plymouth, the Marsh Bar at the Sheboygan Marsh, North Point in Elkhart Lake, Fox's in Oostburg and Pfrang's or Boeldt's and Weyer's in Cascade.

Road trips were made by teens to others just outside the county: Megger's and Steinthal in Kiel, Redwoods Bar in New Holstein, Stoeckigts in Cleveland, Redbird and Timber Lodge in Manitowoc, and Zodiac and San Souse Lounge, Prom and Tropics in Green Bay, the Elbow Room in Mt. Calvary, Club 18 in Campbellsport and the Hollywood Resort at Wolf Lake.

Music was central to the minor bar experience and from the beginning greats like Jerry Lee Lewis, Chubby Checker, Tommy James & the Shondells, Gary US Bonds and Del Shannon rocked the establishments. Great local bands also made the rounds including Jules Blattner, Love Society and Glass Fog. Jam packed dances were usually held on Wednesday, Friday, Saturday and Sunday nights. The cost for the evening included $2 admission for the bands and $2 pitchers of beer.

While most of the country had a legal drinking age of 21 some states like Wisconsin had different rules. After Prohibition, Wisconsin reserved a "local option," allowing municipal governments to set the age for legal beer drinking. As a result, the state was a patchwork of rules and regulations. Milwaukee had closed its beer bars early on in the minor bar experience.

Sheboygan County, one of the state's so-called "beer islands," became a destination for traveling underage teens who would come to get their fill of alcohol before taking to the highways and returning to their dry hometowns.

A Sheboygan Press article dated May 12, 1967 reported that an ID check at

Weiler's in Port Washington showed in a three hour period that of the 375 checked, 300 were from the city of Milwaukee.

Summer evenings created extra work for local police. Frequent calls from the bars usually involved minor thefts from cars; Eight-track tapes, cash and clothing commonly disappeared. But, fights were also inevitable. Where beer and young men meet, conflicts occur.

Humorously, a May 10, 1969 Press article reported that pranksters picked up a Volkswagon and set it upside down in The Patio's parking lot. William Rose of Kohler was the startled owner. He told investigating officers he parked the car on the lot about at 11 pm that Friday and when he left the Patio to go home at 12:45am he found the vehicle resting on its roof. Rose and several friends righted the car and found only the right rear fender dented.

The Wisconsin tradition of beer bars ended on March 22, 1972 when a new law giving 18 year olds full rights including the right to drink hard liquor in bars went into effect. With this law beer bars ceased to exist. From that time until 1984 it was legal for anyone 18 years of age or older to purchase and drink beer and booze.

In 1974, the Press reported that Harold's 23 Club in Sheboygan Falls was the largest beer bar in Sheboygan County at the time. It averaged five to six hundred people on Friday and Saturday nights. With a $1 cover and 40 cent beers, it was profitable business.

Pressure to raise the drinking age continued through the early 1980s. Effective July 1, 1984, a bill created a drinking age of 19 and then finally in September of 1986 it went back to age 21. But, there was an exception for those who were between ages 18 and 21 on the effective date of the law. Wisconsin 19- and 20-year-olds were "grandfathered in", so in effect, the state did not have a uniform age of 21 until September 1, 1988.

Many may fondly recall the cries of Everyone Out!, Last Call for Alcohol! and the two in, two out capacity routine at the Marsh Bar. It was an era to remember, but all are gone now, and most likely it's for the best.

At left: Ads for weekend entertainment at county minor bars, Sheboygan Press, August 14, 1970.

Below: Ad for The Patio once located on the southeast corner of Hwys Y and O north of Kohler, April 14, 1971.

Below: Weiler's in Port Washington

Heyn's 23 Club, later known as Schmitty's and then Harold's 23 Club. Today it's Range Line Inn on Rangeline Road in Sheboygan Falls.

Members of Glass Fog band – Doug McDade, Tom Kellner, Randy Schwoerer, Dennis Hill.

Kiddies' Camp Serving the Community Since 1926

For eight weeks every summer, starting right after the 4th of July, kids in need of a little added loving care journeyed to Evergreen Park's Kiddies' Camp. Started in 1926, Kiddies' Camp was spearheaded by Charles E. Broughton and helped by his connection with the Wisconsin State Elks Association.

Broughton was passionate about helping the city's undernourished children who had a good meal daily at school, but might not receive proper food during the summer because of families' circumstances.

Kiddie's Camp was actually a spin-off of the city's fresh air school which had dealt with underprivileged kids who were at risk of tuberculosis and disease.

That inaugural group of 21 seven to twelve year olds were recipients of the beneficial treatment the camp afforded. It was hoped that a summer of healthy living, rest and fun would help the campers build muscle and bone and put on pounds of valuable weight. Yes, that's right gain weight!

Three to four pounds was average, seven or eight was something to be celebrated. But, along with this weight gain, which the children really needed, came improved all around health. Doctors and nurses monitored the kids, dieticians planned meals and snacks, experts led play and exercise.

The first camp was quite primitive; lighting was furnished by kerosene lamps, water came from a pump and outhouses were the norm. It was located in the southwest corner of Evergreen Park in the city of Sheboygan.

The children were chosen by the city health officers with the aid of city and school nurses. Kids came because of malnutrition, chronic ailments like asthma or heart disease, close contact with tuberculosis and recovery for a debilitating illness.

Charlie Broughton launched the first fundraising campaigns for the camp, utilizing his podium as Editor of the Sheboygan Press to promote this cause. He sent personal letters to key donors and worked his magic to gain financial support. He was such an advocate of the camp that he was affectionately known as "Press Daddy" to the kids. Broughton worked with Elks' Clubs throughout the state to start camps in other cities.

The camp size grew to accommodate 65 kids. Electric lights were added in

1933. Bathrooms were added in 1936. In 1938 the camp site was enlarged again and a handicraft program was started. Donations of crayons, coloring books, games, paint, paper dolls were received from McClellans, Kresge's and Nelson's Paint Store.

Every day the kids consumed lots of milk, supplied by local companies, and fruit from local orchards at camp. In August 1940 lucky campers were sent home with a one pound box of candy and a dollar bill courtesy of Mrs. Peter Reiss.

Everyone in the city got involved. Recreation Department employees visited twice each week to supervise baseball games. Librarians from Mead Library visited on Fridays for story hour or to show a good movie. Members of the Sheboygan Jaycettes visited every Monday and Friday afternoon to entertain the children with their famous puppet shows. The puppeteers were a highlight of the camp.

A Kiddies' Camp Foundation was also formed in 1945 to provide long term funding for the camp.

After thirty years, the purpose of Kiddies' Camp began to shift. In 1958 the camp saw its first campers with cognitive and physical challenges. Those children attended a two-week day camp to work on life skills and just have fun. In 1964 the facility transferred proprietorship to the Sheboygan County ARC.

Eventually, the name of the camp was changed to Camp Evergreen in the 1980s to better reflect the camp's commitment to young and old alike.

In 1990 a beautiful new 7,500 foot structure was constructed replacing the 1926 building which was built during the Great Depression as a WPA project.

Today the camp is still active and serves the public by concentrating on children and adults with cognitive and emotional issues. It manages adult day programs and weekend camps, some overnight. Each camp and program is designed to fill a pressing need in the County.

Since its inception in 1926 as Kiddies' Camp the program has changed lives in positive ways. It is a true community gem.

Above: Taken July 3, 1934 this is a view of the entrance to Kiddies' Camp at Evergreen Park in Sheboygan, started in 1926 by an effort led by Charles Broughton, Sheboygan Press editor, and the Elks' Club of Wisconsin.
Below: Sleeping accomodations at Kiddies' Camp. This image was taken on July 7, 1931.
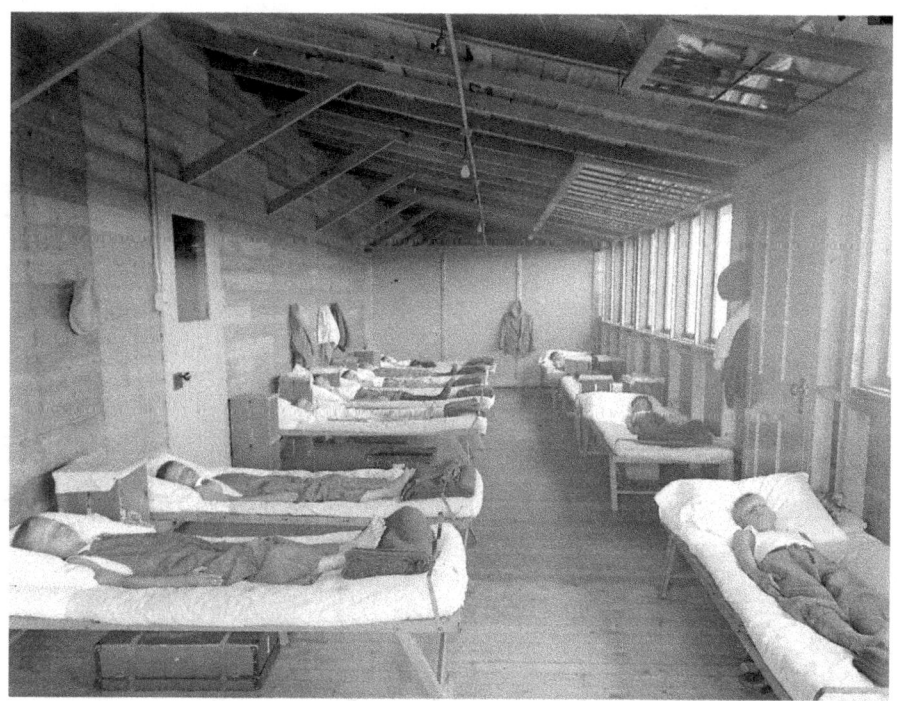

Campers played every afternoon in the sunshine. The camp sported a full array of equipment like the slide and swing sets. The swings image, above, was taken in 1931 and the slide, below, in 1943.

Rhine Center and its Screaming Eagle

Deep in the town of Rhine stands a 12-foot marble monument honoring twenty-three young men from Company B who gave their lives 150 years ago fighting for the Union during the Civil War.

Dedicated on July 4, 1868, this monument was topped with a golden eagle immortalizing Old Abe, a tenacious real-life mascot that was carried into battle by the 8th Wisconsin Regiment during the Civil War. The 8th Wisconsin included Company B Sheboygan County independents.

Old Abe, named for Abraham Lincoln, was a young bald eagle captured near the Ashland-Pierce County line in 1861. The boys in Company C scraped together $5 and bought the eagle as their mascot- a move that would bring the 8th the nickname, The Eagle Regiment."

When the regiment arrived at Camp Randall in Madison, the eagle, overcome by martial music, sprang off his perch, grabbed a corner of the flag in his beak and helped carry it through the gate and up to regimental headquarters. This was a sign of things to come.

The 8th went into action soon after arriving in St. Louis in 1861 participating in a skirmish against Confederate bands near Fredericktown, Missouri. Old Abe sat out the action chained to the courthouse roof, about a half mile from the battle scene, screaming and clawing at his perch.

After wintering at Sulfur Springs, Missouri, the first real battle for the Eagle Regiment came in the spring of 1862 at Farmington, Missouri. After Shiloh, the regiment moved to Corinth, Mississippi, where Old Abe broke his tether during a battle and got into the thick of the fighting. The eagle soared high over the action, screeching all the while, inspiring his soldiers.

Having become so attached to their mascot, members of the 8th took no chances on losing him. Once they even held up an entire line of marchers until Old Abe could be located.

The eagle accompanied the 8th throughout the siege of Vicksburg and on the Red River Expedition in Louisiana in the spring of 1864. Afterwards the regiment and its now famous eagle returned to Wisconsin on furlough.

Old Abe is credited with being present in forty-two battles and skirmishes. Confederates tried in vain to capture or kill the "Yankee Buzzard" as he was referred to, realizing the demoralizing impact it had on their regiment. The reward for his capture or death was larger than that for a number of Union generals.

Six men served as Abe's bearer during the Civil War; three were shot while carrying the eagle on his perch in battle.

Old Abe retired from active duty on September 28, 1864 when he was presented to the state of Wisconsin, his headquarters in a large cage in the basement of the State Capitol after the Civil War.

The bald eagle participated in recruitment events and veterans' parades. He was a champion for fund raising causes. All of this done while sitting on his shield perch attached to a wooden pole. Thousands of photographs of the bird were sold to raise money for soldier relief.

In the spring of 1881 the eagle's long record of service to the state and nation ended. A fire broke out in the Capital basement in March creating an enormous amount of smoke that enveloped Old Abe's cage. Although attendants rescued Old Abe apparently undamaged from his cage, the bird never recovered from the effects of the smoke and died on March 26.

The eagle was then stuffed and placed on display at the State Capitol War Museum. There it remained until February 1904 when an early morning fire swept the Capitol and destroyed much of the museum, including the remains of Old Abe.

Today we still see Abe's likeness on the shoulder patch of the 101st Airborne Division of the U.S. Army.

The town of Rhine monument, located at the intersection of Rhine Road and County Rd FF, ranks second oldest in the state, gaining approval just two years after the end of the war. Unfortunately the original bronze eagle along with one of the two cannons was lost to vandals and had to be replaced with a cast-iron model which was placed on the monument only for Memorial Day and then removed to prevent its theft. But, about the year 2000, a sturdy concrete eagle was crafted and cemented to the top of the monument. That should stay put for a while.

The Rhine Center memorial is a beautiful and thoughtful site to visit.

Stop in at the Historical Research Center, 518 Water Street, Sheboygan Falls, to discover more about Old Abe, the town of Rhine memorial and Company B. Thanks to Mr. Frederick Horneck for much of this information.

Above: Rhine Center monument sketch, originally found in the 1875 Sheboygan County atlas. Located at the intersection of County Roads E and FF, it ranks second oldest in the state of Wisconsin. Below: Old Abe, the mascot of the 8th Wisconsin, Company B, Independents Union soldiers.

Above: Wisconsin State Capitol fire in 1904.
Below left: George Gilles with Old Abe after the Battle of Hurricane Creek, Abe's last skirmish.
Below right: the 101st Airbornes' Screaming Eagle patch.

Joyland, 1950s Summer Entertainment

Summer entertainment for kids has changed a great deal in the last five decades. A favorite childhood field trip that's disappeared are the little neighborhood amusement parks that once dotted the country.

Pony rides, miniature trains and beautiful carousels were standard fare when children's amusement parks first appeared in the 1920s. Kiddie Park, established in 1925, outside San Antonio, Texas proclaims itself to be the oldest children's amusement park. It has survived by preserving its 1920s style and by maintaining all of the original rides.

Kiddieland, perhaps the best known kids' park was located in the Chicago suburb of Melrose Park. Starting out in 1929 with six ponies, it offered rides as an escape for parents reeling from the Great Depression. But, it met its end in 2009 when it was closed to make way for a new Costco.

Sheboygan had its very own kids' amusement park for a short time from 1952 to 1956. Named Joyland, it was located in Evergreen Park across from the quarry on Calumet Drive.

A Sheboygan Press article from May 29, 1952 announced that "Joyland consisted of five rides and refreshments and was owned and operated by George Thompson of Sheboygan." It was later run by Leroy Schrader and his wife, Nellie. The Schraders were veterans of the Dory Miller Show, a traveling circus, he was a canvas man and she was a trick rider.

Joyland was open every weekend. Rides were 9 cents and 14 cents. Every Friday was penny day if you brought four of the following paper cartons of Verifine products: skim milk, orange drink, chocolate drink and buttermilk. By 1956 Fridays were five cents.

The five rides were a roller coaster called the Little Dipper, a merry-go-round, a miniature steam train, boat rides and pony rides. A Ferris wheel was later added. With the exception of the train and the roller coaster the rides were all just for children. The train and the roller coaster could accommodate adults.

Three ponies were available that first year. Over time ownership of the ponies and management of the park were taken over by Jack Grandlic.

The boat rides were taken in small crafts afloat in a large aluminum tank containing 1900 gallons of water.

The merry go round accommodated 24 children. It had 20 horses and 2 sleighs. Although the horses were small in stature, the sleighs could handle adults.

An exact replica of a large locomotive, the engine of the Evergreen Park Joyland Railroad burned real coal and traveled one-half mile each trip. Tracks for the mini railroad covered one-fourth mile on the grounds but two circuits were made for each ride. It had a little water tower and its own tender. There were no covers for the train cars, so coal pieces and smoke would occasionally assault the riders in the first few cars.

Thompson had eight assistants among them a couple named Hank and Ruth. Hank ran the train. Cotton candy, cold drinks, popcorn and ice cream were available for hungry riders.

Thompson had a career as an elephant trainer for many years, he appeared in Hollywood and vaudeville productions with his elephants met his wife when he came to Sheboygan with the circus. The elephants were sometimes part of the fun at Joyland shaving each other with whipping cream and a giant wooden razor.

The kids from Kiddie's Camp were regulars at Joyland because Mr. Thompson generously presented 1800 tickets for free rides to the camp.

Joyland experienced financial problems by 1955. The city agreed to slash its fee for property rental from 13% to 5% of gross earnings. But, by this time it was too late.

The popular park closed in 1956. Its finale came over Labor Day Weekend of 1956. Great advertising managed to fill the last weekend to capacity, but it was too late to turn things around financially.

Sheboygan had a second kids' amusement park located on Superior Avenue just north of today's Randall's Restaurant. Owned by Harry Hummitzsch it lasted a bit longer than Joyland.

Fond du Lac's Lakeside Park is one of the few remaining children's parks in the area. It has a beautiful carousel and train rides for children and a petting zoo in the summer much like the Joyland of old.

Thanks to Jack Grandlic for material for this article. Don't forget to visit the Research Center, 518 Water Street, Sheboygan Falls for more information.

Joyland's roller coaster, above, pony rides, at left and carousel, below.

Cedar Grove Celebrates Its Dutch Roots

On a hot, sunny, Saturday afternoon in late July 1897 a group of first and second generation Hollanders, 48 in number, gathered to celebrate the 50th anniversary of Dutch settlement in Sheboygan County.

Step back in time and imagine some of the conversations at this reunion of friends with a common heritage. Perhaps they spoke of the hardships of the perilous ocean voyage from the Netherlands. Some may have sadly recalled the loss of friends or relatives in the Phoenix disaster that took place just miles from their destination in Sheboygan. Surely they remembered the crude little cabins they hurried to build before that first harsh Wisconsin winter set in. They were certain to discuss how fortunate they were to settle in this area blessed with plentiful wildlife, forests and fertile soil. They likely expressed gratitude for the economic opportunities that were abundant and religious freedom that was assured, the core reasons for their coming to America.

Fifty years later, in 1947, Cedar Grove celebrated its 100th birthday with a four-day festival. This energetic little village threw a huge birthday party! The gala was filled with band concerts, ceremonies and a parade. An elaborate, outdoor Centennial Pageant was the grand finale on each of the first three days of the event: Opening Day, Holland Day, and Homecoming Day. The fitting conclusion to the entire celebration was a community service on Sunday, Worship Day.

The 1947 centennial celebration also marked the first of what went on to become Cedar Grove's Holland Festival. Over the following years, two- day festivals were presented with the American traditions of street scrubbing and klompen or wooden shoe dancing. Parades, musical programs, and operettas including "The Wedding Shoes" and "Tulip Time" were big hits.

In February of 1975 the Holland Guild Gezelschap (Society) was organized to promote, foster, and preserve the heritage of Dutch ancestry within the Village of Cedar Grove in the Town of Holland, Sheboygan County, Wisconsin. It is now the official sponsor of the annual festival.

One of the county's finest summer traditions, Holland Festival is open to the public on the last weekend of July (this year July 25th and 26th). Don't miss seeing the Burgemeester and Town Crier declare the streets clean and announce, "The Holland Festival has now begun."

The parade starts on Main Street at 1:00pm on Saturday. Children perform their Klompen Dancing as part of the opening activities, following traditional street scrubbing.

Klompen, the traditional wooden shoes worn by the Dutch, are donned for dancing, street scrubbing and a children's race. The roomy wooden shoes were originally worn by the Dutch to work in the fields where they protected them from the cold and the moisture. Klomping down the street to accordion music is said to be reminiscent of Dutch ancestors congregating on old cobblestone streets to attend a village event or church gathering.

Today as area residents and guests line the streets of Cedar Grove, where yokes span the broad shoulders of men in Dutch costume as they dip buckets into water barrels, and women and children in Dutch costumes scrub the village's Main Street, be sure to be there to celebrate with our local Hollanders.

This year the book, Cedar Grove, Wisconsin, 150 Years of Dutch-American Tradition, has been updated and reprinted. Three new chapters entitled, Historical Update, Old News and The Royal Visit have been added. The new publication will be available for sale at a discounted price during the festival at the following locations: Holland Festival Souvenir Stand, Het Museum, Te Ronde House Museum, Oma's on Main Restaurant, Cedar Grove Library and the Union Dollar General Store.

Before you leave Cedar Grove be sure to step into the past at Het Museum on Main Street and see Dutch memorabilia and early household and commercial artifacts from the settlements at Cedar Grove and Amsterdam. Incorporated as part of Cedar Grove's museum adventure is the restored TeRonde House, built in 1875 and furnished with pieces form the 1920s and 1930s. It is also open this festival weekend for tours.

Holland Festival, a family friendly event, will be sure to impress visitors with a sense of the courage and resolve of the first settlers, and will communicate the deep love these people had for their homeland, the Netherlands. Zie je daar! See you there.

Holland Festival Street Cleaning - Residents dressed in Dutch costume watch as a young man takes his first swipe at street cleaning.

Holland Festival Kinder Dansers on Van Altena Avenue

Holland Festival –
the Klompenhouwer or the wooden shoemaker demonstrating his craft.

New Cedar Grove books available at Holland Festival this year.

Sheboygan County's Tenuous Ties to Public Enemy #1

On July 22, 1934, John Dillinger, Public Enemy #1, was killed in a shootout with federal agents as he left the Biograph Theater near Lincoln Park in Chicago.

When the Dillinger gang started its crime wave in September of 1933, banks were failing, nearly 4,000 that year alone, stealing the life savings of millions of people. Those that survived foreclosed on tens of thousands of homes, farms and businesses as the economy tanked. With no love lost for the banking industry as a whole, the hoodlums who robbed them were not particularly reviled. There was even a sense of appreciation when the gangsters destroyed mortgage records at banks they hit.

In little more than a year, John Dillinger and his gang robbed several banks, escaped from two jails, eluded police traps and killed at least one police officer. Dillinger mania and fear abounded.

On March 13, 1934 the Sheboygan Press reported that Oostburg resident Jack Fass would be relieved if Dillinger was caught. Fass who happened to bear a striking resemblance to Dillinger was inconvenienced half a dozen times by being mistaken for the criminal. He commented that, "thus far he has been able to convince his "captors" that he is not the man they are seeking." But, in Milwaukee the previous week he had been stopped twice. The second time after five policemen cornered him with revolvers drawn. Mr. Fass confessed that the identity issue had passed the amusing stage and had become something of an ordeal.

Dillinger's gang terrorized the Midwest, mostly in Indiana and Illinois, but a handful of legitimate sightings in Wisconsin caused a great deal of excitement. In April of 1934 the gang needed a remote place to hide out. They found a small summer resort in northern Wisconsin, near Manitowish Waters, called Little Bohemia. It had been built a few years earlier by an immigrant who was friendly with bootleggers and gangsters. But, after a short stay the gang was confronted by Melvin Purvis and the Justice Department. A crazy gunfight ensued and Dillinger escaped, once again.

Never one to be without a woman, Dillinger had multiple girlfriends, among them, Evelyn "Billie" Frechette. Billie's first husband was a man named Welton Sparck, the son of Henry Sparck and Mamie Quast of Sheboygan.

Young Sparck was a challenge from the beginning. In and out of jail much of his life, he reached the criminal big leagues when he, along with two others, robbed postal stations in Chicago in 1932. The three men got less than $200 for their efforts, but because the robberies were federal crimes, the men were sentenced to 15 years in prison at Leavenworth, Kansas and Alcatraz in San Francisco. Sparck married Frechette just before he was sent to Leavenworth, but the honeymoon ended quickly.

Soon after her husband went to prison, Billie met John Dillinger at a nightclub on the north side of Chicago. She told True Confessions magazine (after Dillinger's death and her imprisonment) that as a result of Welton's incarceration, she had a "blurred attitude toward life," She said of Dillinger, "There was something in those eyes that I will never forget. They were piercing and electric, yet there was an amusing, carefree twinkle in them, too. They met my eyes and held me hypnotized."

There it was, a Sheboygan man's wife became the girlfriend of the notorious John Dillinger. Frechette traveled with Dillinger and his gang while they robbed banks. She even once drove the get-away car, but all good things must come to an end and on March 31, 1934, the FBI cornered Evelyn Frechette in a St. Paul apartment.

She finished two years in prison in 1936, then toured the United States with Dillinger's family for five years with their "Crime Did Not Pay" show. She married and returned to the Menominee Indian Reservation in Wisconsin, where she was born. She died in 1969.

After Sparck was released from prison he remarried and had children.

Twenty-three people died of the heat that July 22, 1934, but the death that drew the most attention was that of the Indiana man who, on his birthday a month earlier, had been declared Public Enemy No. 1 by the FBI.

And now you know rest of the story and Sheboygan's tenuous but interesting connections to John Dillinger.

Thanks to Steve Gallimore for the Sparck-Frechette connection.

At right, John Dillinger WANTED poster with its $15,000 reward.

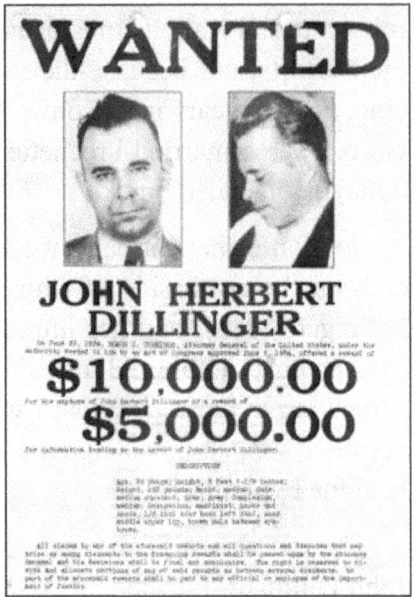

At left, Welton Sparck and Billie Frechette.

At right, Welton Sparck's mug shot

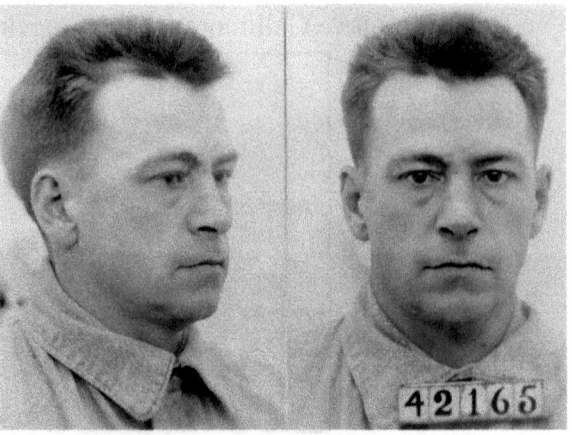

At right is the Biograph Theater on Lincoln Avenue in Chicago shortly after John Dillinger died in a shootout with the FBI. He and two women had just seen *Manhattan Melodrama* at the theater.

Sheboygan Press Headlines on July 23, 1934.

The Sausage that made Sheboygan Famous

Since 1953, August brings Bratwurst Day, a celebration of sausage and of our collective German heritage. The brat is a social food in Wisconsin where Germans first introduced it to the New World. We have brat fries on weekends like folks have BBQs in the south and Chicago has its deep dish pizza. It is part of a deep food tradition.

But, in Sheboygan County, the sausage is something more; it is noble; it is a type of Teutonic soul food. One oldtimer described his perfect day, "We would fry some bratwurst and put them on Hirsch's semel and have a few bottles of Schreier's beer. After lunch we would play horseshoes. It was a feast and a day fit for a king."

Nearly 47% of all Sheboygan County residents claim German ancestry. We have the townships of Rhine and Mosel. We have the Gesangverein Concordia German chorus, D'Werdenfelser Schuhplattlers German folk dance group, the Sheboygan Turnverein (Turners) and Mission House (Lakeland) College started by a band of devout Lippe-Detmolders. And we have the bratwurst.

Few things identify one's German heritage more than making sausage. Sausage was a means of survival for our German ancestors during the winter months, as well as a way to use precious meat scraps and pay homage to their porcine good luck charm.

The real story of German sausage in the county lies, not in Bratwurst Day, but in the small neighborhood meat markets where patrons and owners addressed each other as freund. In the 1940s and 1950s upwards of fifty meat markets fed county residents with a score of sausage types produced weekly.

Heinecke's Meat Market made baloney on Mondays and Thursdays and wieners on Tuesdays. Wednesdays was for Kesselfleisch, a cooked sausage, liver, tongue, braunschweiger, head sausage and blood sausage. Not until Friday did the butcher make summer sausage and bratwurst.

In reality, summer sausage was Sheboygan County's first "star". The Herziger family, who came from Germany in 1839, opened a tavern on the corner of Calumet and Superior in Sheboygan. They also made and smoked sausage at the rear of the tavern. The Herziger Sausage Company, founded in 1916 and by 1952, output went over the two million pound mark. A family story had Grandpa Herziger once proclaiming, "Bratvurst, ach, it vas summer sausage, not bratvurst ve first made."

In the days before refrigeration, summer sausage was superior because it was cured and lasted longer. Brats had to be eaten fresh.

Herziger's was also the first sausage maker to produce all-beef brats. Jewish citizens bought them because they didn't use pork.

Schultz Brothers Meat Market, at 11th and Michigan, opened its doors in 1924 selling five pounds of summer sausage for just $1.00. During cold winters, Elmer Schultz, used hot coals to keep his feet warm as his horse pulled his delivery wagon through the streets. He also held a kerosene lantern between his knees to light the way. Schultz noted that to alert shoppers of the arrival of vendors, butchers had a bell, fishermen a horn and bakers a whistle.

Germans are acknowledged as the premier sausage makers, but Slovenians also made a very popular Kranski Clobasa. Kranski is derived from the Slovenian village of Kranj at the foot of the Julian Alps where the seasonings originated. Luedtke's Food Market made both fresh and smoked Kranski. They typically sold 500 pounds of it during the holidays and another 500 at the annual St. Cyril and Methodius picnic.

Records of brat production are spotty, but we do know that Michael Gottschalk Sr. of Sheboygan began making pork sausages as early as 1862 sometimes roasting them over charcoal fires for his customers. Because of their popularity, they were soon sold to the general public. But, it was years before brat sales surpassed those of summer sausage.

By the 1920s, once ice boxes and later refrigerators were commonplace in homes, bratwurst increased in popularity. From then until the 1960s and 1970s local meat markets flourished and produced tons of bratwurst.

Eateries like Freimund's Brat Stand in Plymouth and Joe Spatt's in Sheboygan popped up in the 1940s and 1950s to sell the grilled wonders.

In 1953, the first brats rolled off the grill at Milwaukee County Stadium, introducing them to the nation. Stadiums across the country soon followed suit, but Miller Park is still the only venue that serves more brats than hot dogs.

To celebrate the city's 100th anniversary, Bratwurst Day was born on Thursday, August 13, 1953. The idea, conceived by A. Matt Werner, editor of The Sheboygan Press, was a means of publicizing Sheboygan's claim to fame: the bratwurst. This wonderful community event was, and still is, sponsored by the Sheboygan Jaycees.

Family-owned meat markets have, for the most part, gone the way of the dinosaur. Government regulations and large supermarkets led to the decline and closure of all but a few. Yet, happily the brat remains. So, as you're enjoying your bratwurst this weekend, remember to salute that very first sausage that made Sheboygan famous, the summer sausage.

Freimund Brat Stand. Shown here in 1957, this unprepossessing stand, located in the parking lot behind Kretsch's Tavern (the Brown Bottle today) near the Mullet River, was a favorite of locals and visitors from 1947 to 1982. (South of Mill Street)

The brat stand was started in the mid-1940s to serve the men who frequented the pig fair that took place in the area. Aaron (Red) and Hazel Miller Kolpin saw the need to provide food for the guys working there. Frank Weilbacher made the original building equipped with just one fryer. Each Saturday and Wednesday, the Kolpins would go to Johnsonville to pick up meat from Ralph Stayer and Carl Hirsh's butcher shop. The brat stand offered charcoal-grilled Johnsonville bratwurst, steak sandwiches, pork loins and cheese sandwiches. Saturday was the busier of the days. Eventually Fridays and Sundays were added.

The first building had no screens, or overhang and was made of wood. After state regulations prompted changes, the building was replaced with one made of sheet metal and other amenities.

Dates are approximate, but it was owned and operated by Aaron and Hazel Miller Kolpin from about 1947 to 1952, Waldemar and Millie Jochmann from 1952 to 1955 and, after 1955, by Otto Freimund and his son Glenweye.

The business was closed about 1982.

Joseph Spatt's Bratwurst Stand: The Come On In was one of the city's first locally-owned, "fast food" restaurants (also known as "lunch rooms"). It served charcoal grilled bratwurst, hamburgers and steaks on semmel rolls garnished with mustard, onions and pickles. Joseph Spatt and his brother, John, operated the popular metal Quonset hut-style eatery on Michigan Avenue for 15 years in the 1930s and 40s. The site is now a vacant lot.

In 1863, Michael Gottschalk opened one of the first meat markets in Sheboygan. He got his start on the north side of the eight hundred block of Michigan Avenue in the former Wendt house, built in 1850. Michael, a Bavarian native, was reportedly the original maker of bratwurst in Sheboygan.

Above: This picture from 1932 is of the Herziger Sausage Company, located at 1228 Superior Avenue. The building in the picture was built in 1924 When Louis wanted to expand his business. At one time, Herziger rented space from Schreier Brewing to dry Sausage. The trucks in the picture were part of a fleet that delivered sausage to Green Bay, Madison, and Racine. Herziger's eventually closed in 1971. Notice the cobblestone street and the small stand to the left of the building, which may have been a forerunner of the fast food drive-thru.

Below: Nic Wagner of Glarus, Russia, came to America in 1913. He owned a meat market in Detroit before moving to Sheboygan in 1928. At one time, a fleet of fifteen refrigerated trucks were used to deliver sausage around the state. Wagner's produced up to twenty different types of sausage, including beerwurst, teawurst, New England ham sausage, and Jagtwurst.

Above: This building at 1435 Indiana Avenue was the home of Rammer Meat Market. Starting in 1904, H. T. Rammer butchered farm animals on site. According to a Sheboygan Press article, one particularly rambunctious bull needed three men to get him into a pen behind the store.

Below: Luedtke's expanded to this building in 1950. An in-store smoke house supplied them with meat until 1972. At its peak, Luedtke's smoked nine tons of hams at Easter and eleven tons at Christmas. For 82 years, Luedtke was the place to get such specialties as rice sausage, headcheese, blood sausage, and mettwurst.

A-fish-ionado: Helen Shaw was fly-fishing artist

Fly-fishing, a pursuit that combines skill and artistry is thought by purists to be the only legitimate way to catch a fish. Rich in tradition, it is an avocation for millions. The beauty of the water, the solitude, and the skills that this baitless sport requires have made fly-fishing a popular pastime for members of the aristocracy, conservationists and the Hollywood elite.

The sport was first introduced to the modern world by writer, Izaak Walton. His book, The Compleat Angler was published in England in 1653 and though Walton did not profess to be an expert with a fishing fly, his prose and verse celebrates the art and spirit of fishing. Walton is the namesake of the Izaak Walton League, an American environmental organization founded in 1922 that wished to protect fishing opportunities for future generations.

Now you ask, how does Sheboygan County connect to fly fishing? Well, Helen Shaw, the gifted artist known as the First Lady of Fly Tying, lived and worked in Sheboygan for years.

Born in Madison in 1910, Shaw's family moved to the city when she was a child. She often accompanied her father on fishing journeys and early on learned the importance of the relationship between a fly fisherman and his tackle. That knowledge would inspire the young Shaw to quickly learn the trade of tying flies.

A fishing fly is simply a hook that has been outfitted with pieces of feathers, fur, thread, and other materials in order to resemble a fly or other small insect. Flies are tied in over 5,000 patterns and sizes, and each has a specific name.

By the mid-1930s, Shaw collaborated with tackle retailer Art Kade of Sheboygan where he allowed her to explore her knowledge of entomology to produce exceptional flies of her own design.

In May of 1937 the Spring Farm Rearing Club sponsored its first annual conservation exhibition at Eagle's Hall. Thousands of people attended and for the first time women played a pivotal role as exhibitors. Helen Shaw and Beatrice Morken, both tying experts, demonstrated their art for enthusiastic observers.

In 1949, Helen was honored as the world's greatest fly-tier at a banquet of the Sportsmen's Club of America. She was also named to the Fishing Hall of Fame. A March 26, 1949 Sheboygan Press article crowed, "Fly fishermen agree that live flies have nothing on the superb creations of fur, feathers and wire made by Miss Helen Shaw at the Art Kade Flycrafters shop here in Sheboygan."

In 1952, Arthur Kade succumbed to a long illness. A passionate conservationist and founding member of the Izaak Walton League, Kade's ideals influenced Shaw throughout her life. His enthusiasm for the art of angling reaching far beyond his passing through Shaw.

By the time Shaw opened her own studio, her reputation had reached the fly fishing community nationwide opening doors to greater things. Helen struck up a friendship and then a courtship with director of Field and Stream magazine, Hermann Kessler. Once married to Kessler, Shaw moved to New York.

A partnership with Field and Stream exposed Shaw's work not only to the magazine's readership, but to the influential Anglers' Club of New York. Shaw could not have found a more appreciative audience for her abilities. Her flies satisfied the needs of some of the most discriminating fly fishers, including President Herbert Hoover and Norman Rockwell.

Shaw and Kessler worked together to create the 'bible' of the craft. Fly Tying, Materials, Tools and Technique was first published in 1963. Shaw's easily understood text book technique, combined with Kessler's stage by stage photos made the book success. For the first time each photo was taken from the tyer's perspective. The book has been reprinted many times, but remains the definitive resource for enthusiasts.

Shaw's accolades continued throughout her life, but after the death of her husband in 1993, she ceased making flies. Living a reclusive life in her later years, among collectors and aficionados she was affectionately known as the Greta Garbo of fly tying. She just wanted to be left alone. And, like Garbo, she also had a greater impact on her craft than did any other fly tyer.

Helen Shaw lived a private life until her death at 97 in New York in 2007.

Part of Shaw's legacy lives on in concerns like Project Healing Waters Fly Fishing, a program that assists military veterans as they deal with injuries. The program includes fly tying, fly casting and fly fishing. It's run by volunteers and offered free to vets at more than 100 sites in the U.S. As wounded soldiers work with the craft's essentials — vises, bobbins, scissors, hooks, thread, chenille, tinsel, feathers and lead, as well as Shaw's books, they heal. The therapeutic value that comes with the activity creates a sense of accomplishment and a sense of serenity whether standing in a river casting a lure or crafting one in a shop.

Helen Shaw Kessler is truly one of our county's hidden historic gems.

Above left: Helen Shaw with a casting rod. Above: Helen Shaw's book, Fly-Tying, Materials, Tools and Technique and some of Helen's flies:

Below: How-to instructions from the pages of Helen Shaw's book, Fly-Tying, Materials, Tools and Technique.

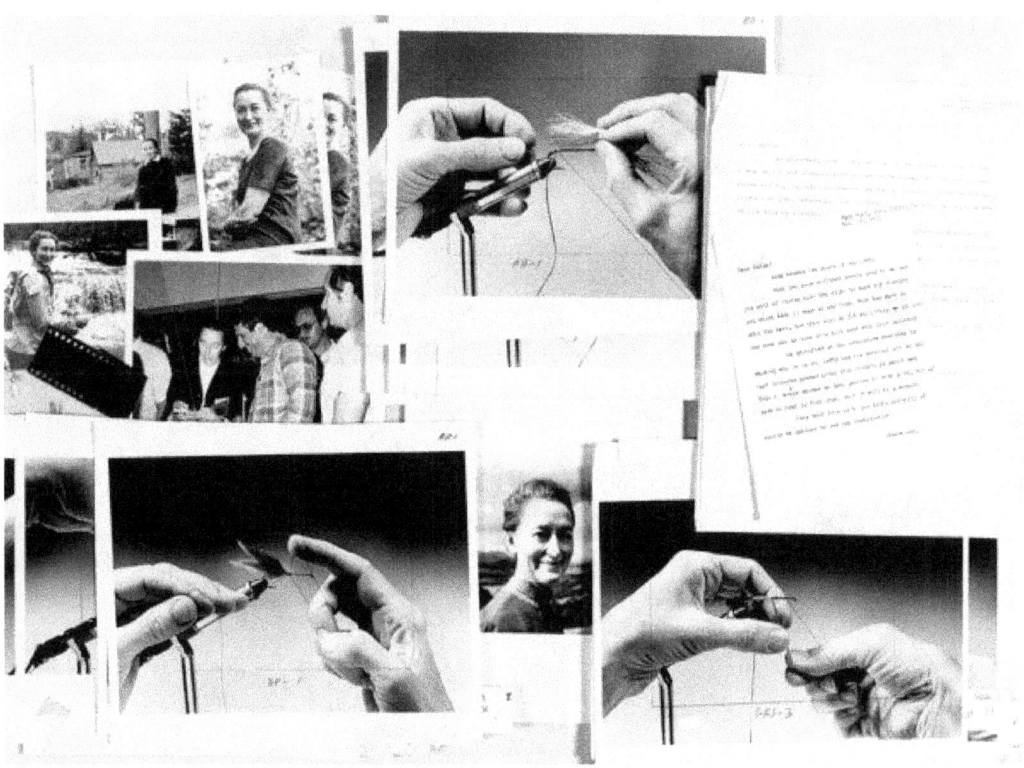

Above: Art Kade's Flycrafters store above Keitel's Candy Store on North Eighth Street just south of the Sheboygan Theater. Below; President Herbert Hoover fly fishing with a box of Helen Shaw's flies.

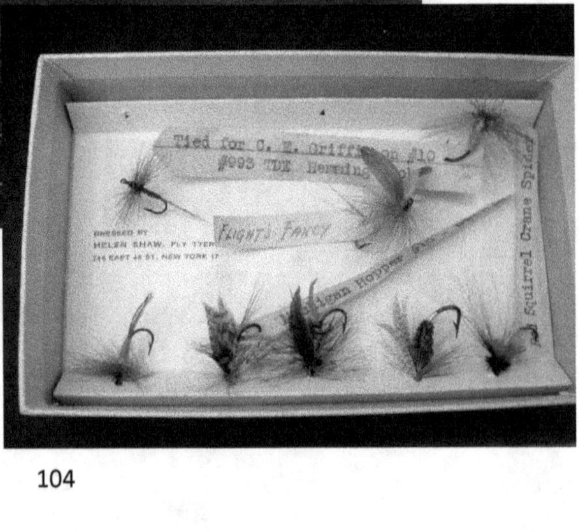

Helen Shaw's fans honor her in many ways. Tim Lawrence, a local artist, created this painting with one of Helen flies featured prominently. Tim's brother, Steve, sent it to Mrs. Shaw when she was about 94 years old and asked her to sign and date the picture and verify that it is her fly. And she did.

Below: The fly is Sedge Ozark, circa 1935 by Helen Shaw

Sheboygan County Supplied Scientists for Manhattan Project

Sixty-nine years ago on August 6, 1945, at 8:16 a.m. an American B-29 bomber, the Enola Gay, dropped the world's first atomic bomb, over the Japanese city of Hiroshima ushering in the Atomic Age. Three days later a second bomb exploded above Nagasaki and a third bomb was ready for release had Japan not surrendered to end World War II.

This was the first time that most Americans knew of the country's great secret, the Manhattan Project. But, in reality, the nuclear age began years earlier. The deadly bombs, nicknamed Little Boy and Fat Man, were the products of years of scientific research done clandestinely.

By 1939 the physics community had good reason to fear the Germans. The discovery of nuclear fission in Germany and the fact that the Nazis were stockpiling uranium from captured Czech mines could mean only one thing: Germany was developing an atomic bomb.

Albert Einstein, Enrico Fermi and Leo Szilard, preeminent physicists living in the United States, agreed that President Roosevelt must be informed of the dangers of atomic technology in the hands of the Axis powers.

Einstein penned a letter to President Roosevelt urging the development of an atomic research program, and even though Roosevelt was only lukewarm to the idea, in late 1941, the American effort to design and build an atomic bomb received its code name — the Manhattan Project.

Headquarters for the project was at 270 Broadway where more than 5,000 people worked on the project in central New York City from 1942-43 in a skyscraper hidden in plain sight right across from City Hall, ergo the name Manhattan.

Though it eventually included over thirty research and production sites, the Manhattan Project was carried out in three main cities: Hanford, Washington, Oak Ridge, Tennessee, and Los Alamos, New Mexico.

After Fermi's staff of physicists produced the first controlled nuclear chain reaction at the University of Chicago in 1942 the project progressed at breakneck speed. Nuclear facilities were built at Oak Ridge, Tennessee (uranium) and Hanford, Washington (plutonium). The main assembly plant was built at Los Alamos, New Mexico and led by Robert Oppenheimer.

In the search for manpower and brains, government recruiters searched everywhere. The recruiters raided university faculties for Ph.D.s and graduate students. At one time, there was a greater concentration of Ph.D.s working on the Manhattan Project than anywhere else on earth. Almost all were under 40.

Seven Sheboygan County residents were part of the war effort. The Sheboygan Press proudly announced their participation in an August 24, 1945 article.

Lyle Brehm of Sheboygan was a mechanical engineer employed by General Electric who worked in the Oak Ridge plant. Brehm commented that they carried bits of photographic film in their pockets to show the amount of radiation they were exposed to and until the destruction of Hiroshima had no idea of the ultimate objective.

Ward Schaap of Oostburg, was a graduate of Wheaton College and a research chemist at the University of Chicago and then Oak Ridge, Tennessee.

John Lohmann, a graduate of Central High, majored in chemistry at UW-Madison. He worked at Kohler Company and A.O. Smith as a chemist until his induction into the US Army in 1941 where he worked at the Edgewood arsenal in Baltimore and finally in advanced electrical engineering at Oak Ridge.

Simeon and Carol Maas Galginaitis were both graduates of Central High and Ripon College. He was a physicist and she, a chemist. Both were recruited for Oak Ridge from du Pont where they worked.

Dr. Roger Voskuyl of Cedar Grove, a professor of chemistry at Wheaton College, studied atomic theory at Columbia University and then the University of Chicago where he helped perfect the atomic bomb.

Dr. Eugene Brimm, Central High grad, received his degree in chemistry from UW-Madison in 1936. He ended up as a research chemist at Linde Air Products.

The first nuclear test named Trinity took place in the desert outside Alamogordo, New Mexico. Everything was done in secret, but, New Mexicans were well aware that something extraordinary happened the morning of July 16, 1945. Windows were shattered 120 miles away in Silver City, and residents of Albuquerque including a blind girl, more than 200 miles to the north, saw the bright light of the explosion and felt the shock waves moments later.

Fear among the scientists was palpable. Despite best efforts no one really knew what would happen or how powerful the blast would be. This was unfamiliar territory, an area with no prior experience.

Technicians at Los Alamos were astonished to hear their project's top physicist,

Enrico Fermi, take side bets on whether they might ignite the entire atmosphere. Col. Groves, the West Point engineer in charge of the full project, told one of his engineers: "If the reactor blows up, jump in the middle of it and save yourself a lot of trouble."

After the final bill was tallied, nearly $2 billion was spent on research and development of the atomic bomb. The Manhattan Project employed over 120,000 Americans, including 7 scientists from Sheboygan County.

Albert Einstein and Franklin Roosevelt, key players in the race to the atomic bomb.

Shift change at the Y-12 uranium enrichment facility in Oak Ridge. Notice the billboard Make CEW count. Continue to protect project information. CEW stands for Clinton Engineer Works, the earlier name for Oak Ridge.

More to the Story

Jean Patrick Manion, another Sheboyganite, was also a part of the Manhattan Project. Manion's wife Huetta Heus Manion shared the following:

"After Jean graduated from UW-Madison he was on his way to the University of Minnesota to begin graduate studies when his trip was interrupted by a call from a U.S. government official who said Jean was needed in research for an important project.

Jean was told to go to the railroad station and ask for Mr. DuPont at the window. He did so and an envelope was given to him that had a ticket to Chicago in it. In Chicago he was instructed to ask for Mr. Du Pont at another window and there was given an envelope to Knoxville, Tennessee. In Knoxville he was given an address to a downtown location and was beginning to suspect foul play. But then, when he arrived at the address he was soon joined by a fellow chemist he knew in college. That started the chain of events that lead to his arrival via a jeep to a complex being built some miles out of the city. The dormitory to which he was conducted in Oak Ridge, Tennessee was accessible from planks laid down on muddy ground.

Once at the dormitory he was given instructions to proceed to an office where he learned about research being conducted there of which he would become a participant. Jean was involved in basic research into the chemistry of plutonium. He is noted in Glenn Seaborg's book "The Plutonium Story."

Two years later he left Oak Ridge for a fellowship at Notre Dame University where he received his Ph.D. in Physical Chemistry in 1951. That same year he married Huetta Heus and accepted a research position with Olin Industries in Alton, Illinois. He later transferred to Allis Chalmers, West Allis, Wisconsin and was research group leader in developing the first fuel-cell powered tractor in 1960. The tractor is part of the Smithsonian Institution collections in Washington, D.C. His research in many areas generated more than 35 patents. "

Sheboygan Press Headlines, Monday, August 6, 1945

Sheboygan County Residents Aided In Atomic Bomb Development

Above: August 24, 1945 Sheboygan Press headlines with photos of seven local scientists who worked on the Manhattan Project.
Below: Centers of research for the Manhattan Project, Oak Ridge, Los Alamos and Richland or Hanford were the three main cities.

Lost and Found in the Canadian Wilderness

As the fate of missing Malaysia Airlines Flight 370 continues to remain a mystery it brings to mind other lost flights. For most, no wreckage or bodies have ever been recovered and the puzzle surrounding them continues. While others, after coordinated searches, turned into successful recoveries.

Glenn Miller, legendary big band leader, was lost on an RAF flight from England to Paris on December 15, 1944. His plane never arrived and was assumed down over the English Channel. But, conspiracy theories abound with this crash. The most peculiar theory had Miller dying of a heart attack in the arms of a French prostitute and the American military covering up the episode. Perhaps the most likely cause, because of a valid witness, had Miller's plane hit in a "friendly fire" accident while bombs were being jettisoned after an aborted raid on Germany.

In June 1950, 58 people lost their lives when Northwest Airlines Flight 2501 disappeared six miles east of Milwaukee over Lake Michigan on a flight from New York to Minneapolis. Boats and planes scoured the lake for a week after the disaster, but with the exception of a small amount of debris and human remains floating on the waters of Lake Michigan, no wreckage has ever been found and no explanation ever given as to the cause of the crash.

So, when on August 9, 1951, Sheboygan Press headlines shouted, "Tasche-Eichenberger Plane Lost," the gut feeling of many Sheboyganites was not good.

Two county residents were missing somewhere in the Canadian wilderness. Dr. John Tasche of Sheboygan and Niles Eichenberger of Plymouth, both experienced pilots, were headed to Stoney Rapids in remote northern Saskatchewan for a few days of fly fishing.

The two men left Sheboygan on July 29 for a two-week trip. Their plane was equipped with plenty of food along with survival equipment, but prior to leaving Dr. Tasche had left instructions with Saskatchewan government officials, "I'm leaving with a full load of gas for Stoney Rapids and then back to Black Lake and possibly Cree Lake, and will wire you on arrival at Stoney Rapids. If you receive no word from me in three days, start a search."

With no communication from Tasche after a week the RCAF (Royal Canadian Air Force) commenced "Operation Tasche", methodically searching the doctor's flight path covering more than 30,000 miles in the first few days.

On August 14th Curt Joa, Dr. Leslie Tasche, John's cousin and Ruth Joa, left

Carm Airfield outside of Plymouth to aid in the search. Both Joa and his daughter were pilots. Joa thought Tasche's plane may have been pushed off course by strong headwinds and run out of fuel. They also planned to hire bush planes to aid in the search.

After scouring more than 90,000 miles of wilderness over 11 days and spending more than $20,000 on fuel, a scarce commodity in the far north, the RCAF search was abandoned.

But, folks at home never gave up. Local citizens rallied to get the attention of Gov. Walter J. Kohler Jr. who managed to restart the search. On August 29th two U.S. Air Force B-17 bombers and two Catalina flying boats joined the search and after just two days a Sheboygan Press headline announced, Find Two Missing Men, Tasche and Eichenberger, Safe and Sound.

The men were sighted by the U.S. Air Force shortly after noon on August 31st on Snowbird Lake in an unmapped part of the Northwest Territories, 128 miles northeast of their original destination.

Missing for 29 long and difficult days, both men were bearded, mosquito-bitten and much thinner.

When asked about the cause of their debacle, Tasche noted their compass spun crazily and ceased to work causing them to wander too far north, past the tree line where they landed on a small unnamed lake. By then their fuel was nearly spent.

They conserved their rations and supplies, eating a great deal of boiled fish. Matches were precious and no more than three were to be used each day, but it was fire that saved them. Each day they lit fire signals. One set on an island in Snowbird Lake caught the attention of an officer on one of the B-17s. As the plane edged closer they could read HELP written in the sand and saw the two men waving their arms. Within two hours Tasche and Eichenberger were rescued.

After a happy reunion with family, the men flew safely back to Sheboygan and ended their journeys to the wilderness of Canada; for once a happy ending to a missing plane.

At left:
Dr. John Tasche of Sheboygan

At right:
Niles Eichenberger of Plymouth

Below: Dr. John Tasche, his wife and daughter are shown preparing to leave home at 2335 North 3rd Street in Sheboygan for a much needed rest. They were bound for an undisclosed cottage to do nothing more than "take things easy."

Above: Sheboygan Press Headline, Friday, August 31, 1951.

Below: Niles Eichenberger, 52 of Plymouth, shown heavily bearded, is greeted by family and friends after the pair's arrival at the Kohler Airport.

In Our Spare Time:
Bowling has been a Sheboygan mainstay

Modern-day bowling traces its origins back to medieval Germany. Menfolk, in order to protect themselves from bands of wandering thieves, carried wooden clubs or kegels. Over time, those kegels also became a source of entertainment. Men would set up their clubs, symbolizing heathens, and throw stones at them. If the kegels fell, the heathens were defeated and the victors would celebrate.

Kegeling or bowling gradually worked its way into mainstream Teutonic life. The church was one of the sports' biggest supporters. It was also a staple at all outdoor events including that of the Turners. Eventually, kegeling moved indoors to kegelbahns. Not suprisingly, they were usually connected with taverns or inns. Hence, the creation of today's bowling alley and perhaps the 'Friday night out' tradition.

The game also shifted from nine to ten pins, conceivably to skirt laws of the mid -1830s banning the nine-pin game because of its gambling element; though why nine-pin is more ruinous than ten-pin is unclear.

Indoor bowling lanes made their debut in America in 1840 in New York City.

Locally, one of the first bowling alleys in Sheboygan was located at 1442 South 12th Street. Built in 1899 by owner Valentine Straus, he bowled a 491 for his first league series with Walter Scherer as his first pin setter. Emil Clarenbach hit the first 300 game here.

Other early venues included Oehler's Alleys on the northwest corner of 10th and Michigan in the early 1890s. There were the YMCA alleys under the old Herr Dry Goods store, later the Fair Store, where the Rex Theater stood at 931 N. Eighth. Diestelhorst Saloon one block south had alleys along with its auspannung or farmers' rest.

Originally balls were wooden. Mottled mineralite and hard rubber balls appeared about 1910. Early on alleys always furnished balls. No one owned their own ball or bowling shoes.

Holy Name Church had a set of alleys in the basement of the school by 1903. Bethlehem Lutheran Church also provided a place for a game of ten pins.

Popular from the beginning, bowling was even used as a marketing tool to bolster the enthusiasm of a Chicago church's flock. An October 30, 1908 Sheboygan Daily Press article, announced Preacher Wants Theater and Bowling Alleys Attached. It seems the Warren Avenue Congregation was suffering from waning attendance and deplorable social conditions. The Rev. Mr. Smith thought his congregation could benefit from some social enjoyment and fellowship.

Another 1908 article mentions Matsui Matsui, the proprietor of the Fortune Bowling Alley at Lake View Park, who was unfortunate enough to be the victim of typhoid, a not uncommon affliction of the time. He mentioned that he hardly every drank lake water. His drink of choice was tea. Matsui lived on Indiana while his family still resided in Japan.

A Sheboygan Press article dated November 18, 1911 boasts that "Alderman J.P. Mannebach, who conducts a saloon on South Twelfth Street, will install four fine Brunswick Balke Bowling alleys." It continues with, "There are a number of good bowlers in the southwest portion of the city who will welcome this good news." Bowling had arrived.

By 1953 there were 17 bowling establishments in just the city of Sheboygan and a dozen elsewhere in the county.

In 1966, Billy Sixty, Milwaukee Journal sportswriter, penned an article about the area's oldest bowling alley. Supposedly, in 1863 a German farmer named George Steinke started Wisconsin's bowling ball rolling in Cascade. Sixty was sure that in the dank cellar of Steinke's farmhouse- a cave they called it- George built two alleys said to be the first in the state.

Research has proven some of this false. The Steinkes, who didn't arrive in Sheboygan County until 1882, did have a bowling alley in one of the sheds on their farm, but not in 1863. They were still in Germany. But, they also had two lanes in the basement of their saloon on Madison Avenue in Cascade by 1919.

George Steinke fashioned wooden balls that changed shape with a turn of the temperature and he made pins that were spotted by hand. Kerosene lamps and candles furnished the light were often blown out by gusts of wind.

Stops or pads at the end of the alleys were made of cornhusks. The balls would "klump, klump, klump" down the lanes, hit the pads and fall off occasionally breaking the crocks of homemade pickles stored nearby. The pungent smell of pickles mixed with tobacco and beer created a not-to-be-forgotten aroma.

Local businessmen from Cascade were the alley's patrons. They might bowl a few frames or take part in the marathon card games held in the cellar. The alleys were torn out during the tenure of Maurice "Red" Hughes in the 1940s.

Gone are Sopetto's in Falls, Casey Jones in Plymouth, Bil-Mar of Cascade, the two lanes in the basement of the bank in Cedar Grove and the Knotty Pines lanes in Oostburg. Though still popular, competition for free time activities is fierce. Facilities remain only in Sheboygan, Pine Grove, Howards Grove, Elkhart Lake and Random Lake.

After more than a century, it seems we have found a different use for our spare time.

Open bowling Friday, Saturday and Sunday, Immanuel hall, 17th and Illinois.

Below: Steinke's bowling alley in rural Cascade.

Above: Alleys at the American Club

Below: Plymouth bowlers, the Red Reubens in 1903, "After the game".

Diestelhorst's Eighth Street Bowling Alley

OUR SPEEDY SPECIALTY
BROASTED CHICKEN

Only one in Sheboygan County. New, scientific cooking equipment turns out golden, tender, tasty chicken IN JUST SIX MINUTES.

½ **CHICKEN**
French Fries, Bun
$1.35

OPEN BOWLING
24 HOURS A DAY
AUTOMATIC PINSETTERS

Chicken Dinners, complete $1.75
FAMILY STYLE
BANQUET PARTIES
$2.25 and up

2 beautiful banquet rooms available

ARNDT'S PLACE
24-HOUR SINCLAIR SERVICE
Hwy. 23 East of Plymouth

OPEN BOWLING
on SATURDAY
and SUNDAY

Johnnie
FOX
BOWLING ALLEYS
1515 New Jersey Avenue
Delicious Food and
Beverages, friendly service

Sheboygan County Meets the Fab Four

Where were you Sunday night, February 9, 1964? Like most of us, you were probably glued to your black and white 14 inch Sylvania watching The Ed Sullivan Show. That night we experienced one of those seminal events that remains crystal clear in memory even after fifty years- the arrival of the Beatles and the beginning of a new chapter in American life.

That night the Fab Four (Paul McCartney, age 21, Ringo Starr, 23, John Lennon, 23, and George Harrison, 20) performed live on Ed Sullivan's variety show reaching an estimated 73 million viewers. That meant that 40% of the U.S. population was watching the same show. They sang five songs: "All My Loving," "Till There Was You," "She Loves You," "I Saw Her Standing There" and "I Want To Hold Your Hand."

Although difficult to hear the performance over the screams of teenage girls in the studio audience, Sullivan knew a good thing and immediately booked them for two more appearances that month.

The Beatles had arrived at Kennedy International Airport in New York two days earlier where they were greeted by 3,000 screaming teenagers. After ten days in America and a handful of concerts filled with fan hysteria, the Beatles returned to England.

Two months later Beatlemania reached a peak during the first week of April when twelve slots on the Billboard Hot 100 singles chart were held by Beatles' songs. 1964 was the year Elvis abdicated his place at the top of the music charts in favor of four lads from Liverpool.

The summer of 1964 also brought great cultural change to America. Teens were anxious to break from the buttoned up, buzzcut lifestyle of the 1950s. The Beatles brought mop tops, great music and good natured social rebellion which was the catalyst for just such a major cultural shift.

By the time the Beatles first feature-film, A Hard Day's Night, was released in August, Beatlemania was epidemic around the world including here in Sheboygan County.

Locally the film was shown as the Wisconsin Theater in Sheboygan. An August 29th Press article headlined 'Screaming Malady Afflicts Teenagers – It's Beatlemania'. Hundreds of teens previewed the flick which was also the Jaycees' Quarry Benefit movie. The Press article reported that the decibel level was beyond description, starting at a high F and taking off for the stratosphere. The plot of the movie was an oddly done, day in the life of. . . but the kids didn't care. The Beatles were there on the big screen right in front of them.

Lynn Siever and friends of Kohler attended the movie premier. Press photographer, Gene Henschel caught them reacting to the film, shrieking There They Are! It's the most! That Ringo! The girls were alternately in and out of their seats, hands covering their faces as they screamed with excitement.

The crowning touch of that summer of 1964 in Wisconsin was the Beatles' concert on Friday, September 4th. The Beatles performed a single show at the old arena in Milwaukee - their only performance in the state.

Landing at Milwaukee County Airport, now Mitchell International, they were taken directly to the National Guard headquarters away from the crowd, leaving behind seven hundred disappointed fans and then were driven to their hotel, the Coach House Motor Inn at 19th and Wisconsin, now a Marquette dormitory.

Tickets, which cost between $3.50 and $5.50, went on sale in April 1964 at the arena box office - remember, no Ticket Master - and within a week all 12,000 had sold out.

The Milwaukee concert began at 8:00 p.m. with opening acts: The Exciters, Jackie DeShannon, Clarence Frogman Henry and the Bill Black Combo. The Beatles performed their usual 30-minute set, arriving on stage shortly after 9pm.

During the show the Red Cross treated at least 10 fainting girls. Kathy Ludwig and Patty Stoelb, both 15 of New Holstein, attended the Milwaukee concert. They managed to see the Beatles leave the venue and gushed that 'George Harrison was so close they could have touched him'. Screaming may have occurred.

That summer of 1964 President Lyndon B. Johnson began his War on Poverty; Plans for a World Trade Center were announced in New York City and the first U.S. report called "Smoking & Health" connecting smoking to lung cancer was released. All important issues, but what do we remember? We remember the Beatles. We still clearly see and hear those four kids from Liverpool who gave us some really great music.

Lynn Siever of Kohler reacts to the Beatles movie, Hard Days Night, shown at the Wisconsin Theater in August of 1964.

Poster of the September 1964 Milwaukee Beatles' concert.

Ticket stubs from the 1964 Milwaukee Beatles' concert.

Falls' Helen Brainard Cole was notable Civil War nurse

The War Between the States (1861-1865) changed the face of Sheboygan County in many ways. For generations after, the sight of wooden-legged and empty-sleeved veterans would cast a sobering note among the gathering places of the community.

But, it also gave one of our local girls the chance to play a part in the drama that was center stage in 1865 Washington D.C.

Helen Brainard was born in 1838 in Oneida, New York. Her family traced its history in the United States back to 1662 with the founding of Haddam, Connecticut. The Brainards moved west to Sheboygan Falls in 1846 where Helen married William Cole, the son of Charles and Sarah Cole in 1858. Marital bliss quickly turned tragic when less than a year later William died from tuberculosis.

With the Civil War raging, and Helen's father and brother already enlisted in the conflict, she was determined to serve her country in some capacity.

Men were the original Civil War nurses as women were generally thought to be too frail to cope with the rigors of caring for the wounded. Yet, thousands of women demanded to serve as volunteers. Very quickly they went from sitting on the sidelines to managing the care of the soldiers. The face of nursing was about to change.

After the carnage of Bull Run, Clara Barton and Dorothea Dix organized a professional nursing corps and Helen Brainard of Sheboygan Falls volunteered. Not yet 21 years of age, her offer of hospital work was refused; only women 30 years and older were accepted.

But, ever capable and persistent, Helen secured an appointment as secretary to Miss Dix, which eventually led her to becoming a nurse at Campbell Hospital in Washington, D.C.

It was there that Helen first met President Abraham Lincoln. Lincoln spent a great deal of time visiting the wounded; Mrs. Cole described him as being everywhere. She remembered him as talking about the soldiers and their suffering and how he wished he could help them. He was so kind, so good and so great.

Always the "ordinary guy", Helen once caught him cutting himself a piece of strawberry shortcake and then sitting down on the floor in a corner to enjoy the treat, perhaps taking a momentary break from his war worries.

When Lincoln's impetuous, wild child, Tad, became ill, Helen was one of the nurses who cared for him. She was even given the gift of clothing by Mrs. Lincoln in thanks for her service.

Helen was a popular figure in Washington and counted many famous people among her friends and acquaintances. Among them were John Greenleaf Whittier, Charles Dickens, Harriet Beecher Stowe, General and Mrs. Ulysses Grant, Horace Mann, Oliver Wendell Holmes, Theodore Roosevelt and Mary Baker Eddy even studying Christian Science under the guidance of Mrs. Eddy.

Frighteningly, she also, just days before the events at Ford's Theater, played the game of Whist with John Wilkes Booth over an afternoon, never imagining what was on his wicked mind.

After the Civil War ended, Helen went to Memphis to close a hospital for African American veterans. Next she worked at a home for "unfortunate women" in Boston.

The health of her aging parents finally called Helen back to Sheboygan Falls. She sold the family home around 1913 and spent the rest of her life living in the Grand Hotel in Sheboygan. There she would sit in her favorite corner of the lobby and greet friends who came to pay their respects.

A familiar figure at all of the local gatherings of Civil War veterans and patriotic and military societies, Helen appeared at all of the state encampments of the Grand Army of the Republic (GAR) and worked hard for their causes.

On August 19, 1931, Helen fell on the stairway at the Grand Hotel and broke her hip. She died a short time later at the fine age of 93.

A granite boulder-style monument honoring Helen was erected in 1933, just two days after she died. It still stands near the corner of Martin Avenue and Calumet Drive in Sheboygan honoring our local girl who was a Civil War nurse and so much more.

At left: Mrs. Helen Brainard Cole at a GAR (Grand Army of the Republic) reunion in 1920s.

Below: The Grand Hotel, once one of eleven hostelries on Center Avenue, was home to Helen Brainard Cole for nearly thirty years. Built in 1890, it was located between Seventh and Eighth Streets. The *Grand Old Lady of Center Avenue* was torn down in 1963 as Sheboygan sought to modernize its downtown.

Located at Calumet Drive and Martin Avenue in Sheboygan, the monument to Helen Brainard Cole says the following: 1838-1931, In Memoriam, Helen B. Cole, Last of Wisconsin's Civil War Nurses, "She Gave the Rarest of Gifts, Herself to the Building of These Organizations." Carl White Camp #57, Sons of Union Veterans of Civil War and their Auxiliary #19.

At left: Dorothea Dix, founder of Civil War Nursing Corps

At right: Tad Lincoln

A Blasters' Blaster
The Legend of Dynamite Bill

Every community has its share of characters, those people that are larger than life and provide more than their share of experiences that eventually become much repeated legends.

One of Plymouth's most colorful characters was George Gardner better known as Dynamite Bill. Born in Door County in 1887, Gardner started his career in blasting at an early age when he became a powder monkey in a stone quarry at the age of twelve. After moving to Plymouth, he blasted stone for farmers around Elkhart Lake. He further honed his skill as he served two years as an army private in WWI with the Rainbow Division's demolition squad. After the Great War he returned to Plymouth and made a name for himself, leading a life that was alternately that of a hermit and celebrity. The following is from an interview done years ago, interviewer unknown.

Two farmers had a sizzling feud going over a big tree stump that straddled the fence between their properties. One wanted it removed, the other didn't. Dynamite Bill paused in his narrative long enough to "ping" a stream of tobacco juice into a galvanized pail a good five feet away. A few droplets of the brown liquid bobbled down his long white beard as he continued, I settled the feud for good. Blasted out one-half of the stump, left the other half intact. A sharp sliver of blue, darting from between his narrowed lids, challenged me to doubt his story.

I didn't accept the challenge. By that time I was inclined to believe anything Mr. George Gardner claimed about his dynamiting feats. Gardner, more popularly known as Dynamite Bill, had already convinced me that he was, indeed, a veritable Paul Bunyan of the blasting profession. Hours earlier, determined to verify a roster of stories about his miraculous skill with almost an affinity for the dangerous tools of his trade, I had knocked on his door.

Over that door hung a sign, stating simply Dynamite Bill. The building, a former cheese factory, was located right next to the downtown section of America's cheese center, Plymouth, Wisconsin.

It looked ordinary enough from the outside. Once inside, though, the ordinary ceased and the fantastic began. From the mammoth potbellied stove (a century old) to the out-moded mahogany back bar attached to one wall, Bill's home was something out of a housewife's nightmare.

Cut up logs flanked the stove. A discarded TV antenna served as a drying rack for an assortment of grey union suits. Pin-up girls of the Theda Bera era- still looking pink and plump in spite of layers of dust, adorned the back wall. A small sink pump and slop jar were the only plumbing facilities in evidence. A dozen hats, one dirtier and more misshapen than the other, clung to the back bar. Although only one dim bulb struggled against the glow of the stove, there were six crusted, ornate chandeliers dangling from the high ceiling. The rosy reflection of the fire reverberated from stacks of shiny aluminum milk cans, hundreds of them in temporary storage for the new cheese factory across the street. I learned later.

The most outlandish sight of all was Dynamite Bill, himself. He stood beside the stove, head cocked to one side, eyes narrowed with suspicion as I approached. He wore a battered felt hat atop his white curls, an ankle –length wool jersey coat, a flannel shirt, neatly fastened with a row of safety pins, ragged blue-jeans, and oversized rubber boots. The temperature near that blazing stove must have been close to 100 degrees.

Dynamite's suspicion melted as I explained my mission, and the lively blue eyes sparkled with delight? Or devilment? A little of both, I decided, listening to one extraordinary yard after another. Some, I had already checked with his employers.

Bill's blasting feats are legion and he is fast becoming a legend; his fame such that his mail requires no other address than Dynamite Bill, Plymouth, Wisconsin.

When the construction of a TV tower outside Milwaukee presented the problem of rock under the soil and other dynamiting experts demurred, the called in Bill to blast a formation.

When Bill dynamited the rails from the Sheboygan's downtown section, traffic streamed by uninterrupted and not a single cracked shop window resulted.

"I used a blanket of tires threaded together with a cable, for cover. The trick is to keep the cover a little above the rails, otherwise the tires will blow sky-high, too, Bill explained. The tires work like fish gills, letting air through, but blocking solid material."

When the ice jam on the Sheboygan River piled up to eight feet under the Penn Avenue Bridge, several years ago, it was Bill who, without aid, crawled out on the treacherous mound and blasted the jam loose.

"The ice-breaking job was nothing compared to the many log jams I released while working with the lumberjacks in Northern Michigan." Bill shrugged off the almost disastrous ducking he'd experienced scrambling off the river of broken ice. "In log jams, I had to jump and ride spinning logs to the center of the jam, set my charge, then get back to shore on those slick, whirling sticks before the explosion. I learned one logger's lesson real good. Never pick a log turning toward the one you're riding, when have to switch. That way, if you slip, you have a chance to climb back on without being squashed to pulp between logs. I didn't dare slip coming back."

Bill's predictions about the effect of his charges were so precise they bordered on the uncanny. When he leveled a 95 foot power plant chimney in Ozaukee County in 1947, the chimney landed in the exact position Bill had outlined before laying the charge.

Complete confidence in Bill's ability was evident in the unconcern with which various establishments pursued their normal business activities while Bill worked. Customers shopped in Prange's Sheboygan store while Bill blasted out a huge portion of the basement beneath them. Not one dish was jarred in the china department adjoining Bill's operations.

He deftly annihilated the concrete steps leading to the Franklin Hotel Bar in Sheboygan Falls, between beers, as his drinking companions continued quenching their thirsts inside, completely unaware of Bill's activity, so quiet and unobtrusive were his operations.

His skill removed the Milwaukee Boston Store's basement abutments without jarring a window display or cracking a showcase glass.

Sixty-one years of dynamiting experience has perfected Bill's techniques beyond those of his contemporaries. With outdated methods, improvised equipment, and a raw courage seldom witnessed in his fellow man, Bill has consistently executed jobs other dynamites wouldn't attempt.

Building a raceway to run water from the Fox River through Kaukauna's Thilmany Pulp and Paper Company's generator station was too risky for seven dynamiting firms approached. An Appleton firm took the contract after several other companies tried their skill, only to find that their methods were causing minor damage to buildings in the area. Bill was called in and accomplished the blasting of a tunnel 86 feet wide and 13 feet deep without disturbing the alignment of the machinery within the plant one iota.

When the old brick building of the Sheboygan Falls Tannery as taken over by a new concern, Bill blasted holes for the extra windows and doors needed.

So ingenious were Bill's methods, government inspectors paid $45.00 per length of pipe removed from Lake Michigan in and underwater cleanup near Manitowoc in 1958, though Bill's asking price had been only $15.00 per length. The problem had stumped everyone else. Bill simply weighted empty beer bottles with lead, inserted a stick of dynamite in each and lowered the bottles into the pipe. The chain reaction set off by the first charge drove the shattered pipe six feet underground. The inspectors had hoped to entice Bill to perform similar jobs in other parts of the United States, but Bill turned them down. Earlier in his career he had traveled all over the states as a dynamiter, but "With one foot in the grave, and another on a banana peel, I kinda like to stick close to home," Bill told me.

That career started as a powder monkey at the age of 17. As recently as 1963, at 76, Bill was still doing the impossible, like razing a church at Holy Cross while its minister watched through the parsonage window, 20 feet away.

One job Bill didn't like, and never would duplicate, was the demolition of a sunken ore vessel in the Sheboygan harbor, many years ago. To accomplish it, Bill had to don a crude diving suit of the period, descend to the bottom of the river and set enough dynamite in the underside of the craft to blast a small hole through which more explosives could be planted. The problem was to sink the ore to a strategic spot at the bottom of the river and break the remainder of the vessel into pieces that would surface and could be easily removed to clear the harbor for passage.

"It isn't the big jobs, though, that cheat most dynamiters of a natural death," Bill contends. "It's the small ones," Like his blasting holes deep enough to sink the poles of a swing set for a neighbor the year before. Bill handled smaller explosions by breaking a stick of dynamite. If the wood pulp in the stick is evenly packed and contains an equal distribution of nitro-glycerin solution, the discharge of minute particles in the breaking will do no harm. If, on the other hand, the pulp is loosely packed in spots and, as a result, over saturated with solution at these points, the bits of saturated pulp falling against a hard surface will result in a lethal explosion.

Bill denied that courage was an important element of his profession. Experience, knowing just how much and where to place dynamite, and never for a moment forgetting it is dynamite, account for his amazing performances. Only once, in sixty-one years of day by day handling of deadly explosives, has Bill been injured. That time, surrounded by a crowd of sidewalk engineers, he allowed concern for his audience to momentarily distract his attention from his own danger. As a result, he had not moved far enough away to dodge a blast of stones and dirt. He spent two months at Wood Hospital for Veterans, in Milwaukee, before his eyesight was back to normal.

The denial of courage is refuted by Bill's war record. He was the only officially listed dynamiter of World War I from Wisconsin. He participated in the Aisne-Marne, St. Mihiel, Meuse-Argonne, and Defense Sector drives as a member of the medical corps in the sanitary train of the 168th Infantry, 42nd Rainbow Division from 1918 to March, 1919. As a result of those eight months of action, Bill was awarded the Distinguished Service Medal for volunteering to rescue a Captain Elleton under enemy fire. The captain lived only long enough to request that Bill be awarded the medal. Bill also claims he was the recipient of the French Croixe de Guerre for his part in blowing up a bridge on the Marne River to halt a German advance. He kept the medals in two safes, locked in the back room, he said but refused to display them.

Further evidence of Bill's courage is in the records of his flamboyant history. Specifically, his adamant stand against the Women's Christian Temperance Union of Plymouth, during Prohibition . . . in spite of his contention that "Women are far more dangerous that dynamite." That his venture into matrimony ended almost as soon as it began could be the foundation of his fearful attitude to the weaker sex. He ultimately lost his battle with the temperance union and was arrested for the violation of the Dry Law in September, 1927, at Waldo, Wisconsin.

"I was framed," Bill bellowed, whenever anyone touched on that arrest. So necessary were Bill's services to the community, officials relaxed Bill's sentence enough to allow him to fulfill his blasting commitments during the day.

Foolhardy, rather than courageous is the term used to describe Bill by many, due, no doubt, to Bill's many frightening practical jokes. Like blowing a stump from beneath a fishing companion who paused for refreshment there. Outside of a scarred friendship, only a few minor scratches and one spilled bottle of beer resulted from that escapade.

Bill and his own unique method of rebelling against a queue at the barber shop. Shearing of Bill's wealth of red curls and beard was a yearly event. Wealth, here denoting not only quantity but $40.00 actual cash the hair brought from a doll factory. To save himself precious time, Bill always carried a stick of dynamite to the barbershop. If all the chairs were occupied, he'd saunter over to the coal heater and casually pop the explosive into the fire.

"You'd never believe how fast that shop could be emptied." Bill chuckled, reminiscing about those occasions. While customers and barbers alike beat a hasty retreat, Bill's calmly settle into his favorite chair. "Most of them never did understand why no explosion occurred." The gleam in his eye was definitely devilment now. "Too dumb to realize that fire alone wouldn't detonate the stick. Those kind take a percussion cap."

Bill had a right to disparage the intelligence of his friends. A few hours conversation with him was enough to convince me that without benefit of a formal education, even at 77 Bill's brilliance, with the scope of his recognizance of current affairs, and his deep understanding of human nature would credit an intellectual. He could speak and write four languages, English, German, French and Bohemian.

Even more amazing than the man's intelligence was his demonstration of artistic talent as a bonafide old time fiddler.

Though he seldom played anymore, Bill's fiddling revealed flashes of professional mastery. He followed his recital with a thought provoking discussion on what constitutes good music.

"The lowly fiddler is no less exalted than the renowned concert violinist," Bill maintained. "If the song springs from the heart of the musician and is expertly translated into pleasing sounds through an instrument, a hoe down is as good music as any complicated sonata."

Fiddling had long been a hobby with Bill. His face flushed with pleasure as he recalled the old days when square dancing was in vogue and no matter what part of Wisconsin he happened to be working in, some Saturday night, there was always a dance nearby. One hilarious tale involved both his fiddling and his long locks.

He'd been working all day on a rough blasting job, and fiddling until two o'clock at a friend's wedding celebration. Exhaustion, enhanced no doubt by the copious amounts of liquid refreshments consumed, overcame him as he left the dance hall. It was fall, but the air was still warm with the glow of Indian Summer. Shucks, Bill thought, why walk all the way home? A shock of grain in a farmer's field nearby looked mighty comfortable. It was. So much so that the heavy dew and dropping temperature never penetrated Bill's slumber. When he awoke in the morning, his beard and his long red hair were frozen tight to the sheaves of grain. Luckily, the proprietress of the dancehall saw Bill's predicament and came running to his rescue. Bill sent her back, the first time, though, Not for anything would he let an amateur's scissors touch his pride and joy. The locks were salvaged with the aid of a bucketful of hot water.

Bill had to abandon his life's work, finally A severe diabetic condition, coupled with other impediments of old age, are relentlessly taking their toll. Just as the modern detonation procedures and mammoth iron excavating robots have diminished the once popular demand for good blasters.

Dynamiting has been a gratifying life, and a prosperous, one for Bill. Rumors that his to eight foot high safes are stuffed with money were denied by Bill, however. "I use them to store my caps," he explained. His earlier reluctance to open those safes to display the war medals made me wonder, though. It is said that a Plymouth banker makes a periodic visit to Bill's to retrieve hoarded checks. The first visit turned up a collection dating back seven years.

Bill also repudiated the ownership of a sizable portion of the property in Plymouth and surrounding area.

"To tell the truth, I did buy houses on all four sides of town." Bill admitted, his blue eyes going wide and bland with innocence. "That way, if I get a little confused after a night out, no matter which way I head, it's always toward my place,"

Bill has little need for property or overflowing safes. His frugal habitat is as comfortable as an old shoe. With his enviable record of achievement, the respect and admiration of his fellow craftsmen, his own sense of accomplishment, he has more worth than man men attain in one lifetime. Long after Bill is gone, anecdotes about his feats will be told and retold. Scarcely a manor construction operation undertaken during the last fifty years in Wisconsin has been accomplished without summoning Bill at one time or another.

"One more thing I want to tell you." Dynamite stopped me as I prepared to leave. "I never once walked away from a charge without repeating the Lord's Prayer."

Courage? Skill? Or faith? Whatever it was, Bill will probably go down in history as the only dynamiter who has survived, unharmed over sixty years of continuous proximity to the unpredictable, lethal ingredient of his tools . . . . nitroglycerin.

Bill's front door

The photos seen here and on the next two pages came from a collection donated to the Sheboygan County Historical Research Center by Wally's Studio of Sheboygan Falls.

The interviewer who garnered this priceless information is unknown.

WWII GIs bring pizza
back to the states, Sheboygan

Pizza, that most divine gastronomic treat, was created in Naples, Italy as a quick and nourishing food for the working class. Available mainly from street vendors, it remained unknown to much of the world until more than 4 million Italian immigrants streamed into the United States from 1880 to 1920.

Gennaro Lombardi opened the first licensed pizzeria in New York's Little Italy section of Manhattan in 1905. Lombardi modified Neapolitan methods when he exchanged wood-fired ovens and mozzarella di bufala for cows' milk mozzarella and coal-fired ovens to feed the large numbers of Italian immigrants in New York City.

Pizza was a food mostly confined to small areas of the Northeast until after WWII when American GIs stationed in Italy returned home with an enthusiastic appreciation of the foods they discovered while in service. Interestingly, in the 1940s, sales of oregano increased by 5,200 percent over eight years due to the surge in popularity of pizza and other Italian foods. Singers like Frank Sinatra and Dean Martin, who were of Italian ancestry, also helped spur sales.

By the 1950s, pizzerias were found in many of America's cities. According to American Heritage, the number of American pizza parlors grew from 500 in 1934 to 20,000 in 1956. Pizza pundit, John Mariani, explained the phenomenon, "Like blue jeans and rock and roll, the rest of the world, including the Italians, picked up on pizza just because it was American."

Small, independent restaurateurs used only homemade mozzarella cheese, marinara sauce, and toppings they themselves created. They kneaded their own elastic dough and tossed the pizza pies in demand by families and friends looking for a cheap meal out. It was a perfect communal food -- no single slices sold. A pizza was something to be shared with others.

A January 23, 1956 Sheboygan Press article had Joseph Sartori of Plymouth speaking on "Italian Cheese and that Pizza Craze," to the Business and Professional Women's Club at the Sheboygan YMCA. Pizza was still new to the citizens of the county. At that time S&R Cheese produced the mozzarella and parmesan cheese needed for those luscious pies. It's hard to remember now, but the streets of Plymouth, smelled for decades, like an Italian kitchen.

The county has had too many pizza joints to mention in this article, but we'll reference a few. Faye's, located on Calumet Drive in Sheboygan and formerly Russo's has been in business since 1957. An early ad boasted, Pizza Pies, made right before your eyes.

Erie Eat Shoppe, in 1958, had a Volkswagon delivery bus that advertised 15 varieties of pizza in three sizes, priced from 75 cents.

Pizza Village at South 8th and Georgia opened in 1961 under the name, Russo's. It was a local hangout for high school students. Tom and Marlene LaBouve changed the name to Pizza Village when they bought it in July of 1967 and for 26 years they owned the restaurant until they sold in August of 1993 to Mary Jo and Bill Benninger.

When Dino's Pizza, Plymouth's first opened in 1962, a small pizza sold for 90 cents and soda was a nickel. Still in business today, it was also the first in town to serve sub sandwiches.

Sheboygan's first Pizza Hut at 14th and Erie was just the sixth in the state, opening in August of 1969 with Terry Matthias of Sheboygan Falls as its manager.

By 1975 pizza was a staple for teens. Other favorite haunts included Brat'n Burger Pizzeria on North 15th and Pizza Barn on Penn Avenue in Sheboygan. Plymouth also had Mike's Pizza Parlor and Sheboygan Falls had R-Dee's Restaurant and Pizza.

Coming almost full circle, Il Ritrovo of Sheboygan is today known for its certified Neapolitan pizza, and utilizes a wood-fired stone oven, much closer to those used in Italy two hundred years ago.

Pizza sales is a $36 billion per year industry with more than 72,000 pizzerias in the U.S alone. Each man, woman and child eats an average of 23 pounds of pizza yearly. Statistics certainly prove that pizza has evolved from a regional dish of the working class to a favorite of the masses.

So while October might be known for its candy corn and Halloween treats, it is also National Pizza Month, a time for celebrating the America's favorite food. Whether it's pepperoni or cheese, sausage and mushroom, thin crust or deep dish, when next you enjoy a slice, remember to thank the GIs who brought it home.

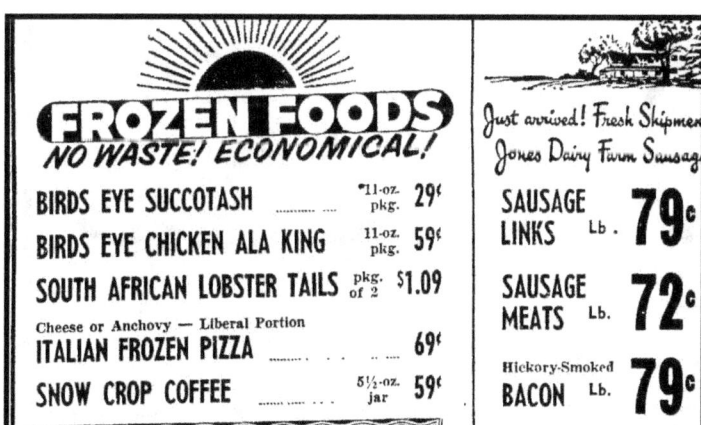

Frozen pizza ad from Fessler's grocery store
1952
Cheese or Anchovy
69 cents

Above: A Sheboygan Press ad featuring Erie Eat Shoppe's Volkswagon Pizza Delivery Bus in 1958. Erie Eat Shoppe was located just east of 14th Street on Erie Avenue.

Below: A February 14, 1953 ad in the Sheboygan Press for a special Valentine's Day meal at the Inn Supper Club once located at 8th and Penn in Sheboygan. Pizza and other Italian dishes were featured.

Above: Faye's Pizza located at 1821 Calumet Drive in the city of Sheboygan. This photo taken in 2014 after a major renovation.

Below left: A 1957 Sheboygan Press ad for Mullen's Appliance sale featuring pizza as a snack and pizza making lessons from home economist, Miss Eleanor Loos. Below right: An image of Russo's, the predecessor of Faye's on Calumet Drive.

Above: Pizza Village was located on the southwest corner of South Eighth Street and Georgia Avenue. Top left: John LaBouve, 1970. Bottom left: Counter at Pizza Village, 1970 and Tom LaBouve, on the job, January of 1974.

Pizza Hop To Be Held Wednesday

CYO of St. John the Baptist Church, 215 West Main St., Plymouth, will sponsor a Pizza Hop and Mardi Gras fiesta Wednesday evening, for teenagers, at the church auditorium. The fiesta will be the final dance before the Lenten season.

Officers have secured the services of Denny and the Crown Jewels of Sheboygan, to furnish music for dancing, which will begin at 7:30 o'clock and continue until 10:30 p.m. A pizza lunch will be served during the evening.

The newest in entertainment for CYO, the Pizza Hop. Sheboygan Press article, spring of 1959.

Above: Pizza Village recently opened at Nonna Maria's at Eight and Georgia in Sheboygan. Below: Newly renovated Nonna Maria's Restaurant. Next page: Interior images of Nonna Maria's.

North to Alaska

In October 1867 the United States grew exponentially in size when it bought the territory of Alaska from the Russians. For $7.2 million dollars ($121 million today) the country acquired 586,412 square miles of land, land more than twice the size of Texas, for less than 2 cents an acre.

In spite of the great bargain, the American citizenry was less than enthusiastic. They believed the land to be unproductive and worthless. The land purchase was christened "Seward's Folly" after William Seward, President Andrew Johnson's hard-hitting Secretary of State who had negotiated the deal with Russia. Yet, when gold was discovered in a tributary of the Klondike River in 1896 public opinion turned more favorable. Alaska might just be a land of promise.

In 1934, Alaska again became a land of promise, when as part of Franklin Roosevelt's New Deal plan to help move the United States out of the Great Depression a number of rural rehabilitation colonies were established. Matanuska Valley Colony at Palmer, Alaska was one of those. It originally consisted of 203 families who bought tracts of land from a 260,000 acre parcel. Families from Minnesota, Wisconsin and Michigan were recruited because of the similarity in climate and the extremely high percentage of residents on federal relief. The Great Depression hit hard in the Upper Midwest

Families were offered 40 acres of land, a barn, house and equipment to settle the valley and farm the land. These "gifts" were to be paid back over a 30-year period beginning in 1938.

Four families from Sheboygan County- the Gus Scheibel family, Sheboygan Falls; the John Herman family, Plymouth; the Edgar Carmen family, Elkhart Lake; and the Burton Gessler family of Sheboygan Falls left to join the colony in May 1935.

The Minnesota and Michigan contingents were the first group of settlers to arrive at Matanuska along with the crew of builders for the settlement. Wisconsin colonists arrived two weeks later. All were transported across the United States by train to Seattle and then by boat to Seward, Alaska.

Wisconsin people, 353 in all, departed from Green Bay by train. Along the route, the colonists were treated like royalty. Arriving in Seattle each was given a red ribbon printed "Wisconsin to Alaska" and a blue one which said "Matanuska Pioneers.

On May 18, the colonists boarded the ship, St. Mihiel. It carried 573 passengers, a full crew, 3,600 tons of freight, 48 dogs, 4 ducks, 2 cats and one canary. There were also four school buses, flooring, roofing and 7,000 tons of freight for the colonists. On May 22 the ship docked at Seward.

Although homes and barns were supposed to have been built, they were not. Families spent their first months in Alaskan in tents. Some of the colonists left immediately upon arrival in the Valley. By March 1939, 537 people in 124 families, or 61 percent, were gone. In 1949, only 63 families, about one third of the original colonists, were still living in the valley.

Advance planning was poor. Many of the basics needed for the community were missing, with no electricity, little water, no churches and no schools. Yet, planners in Washington decided that each farm family should have a modern milking machine. Two hundred machines were shipped, and of course, charged to each family, but they sat unused due to lack of electricity.

Within weeks of the arrival in Alaska, there was a measles epidemic that spread throughout the colony. With no permanent houses or hospitals, and though only a few settlers died, the event was disheartening and foreshadowed the difficulties of living in a remote area. The harsh conditions took their toll on the settlers. In 1965, there were only 20 families left.

Trial and error taught the farmers which crops would grow during the short Alaskan season of almost total daylight. Potatoes, turnips, barley, cabbage, squash and many species of flowers flourished and grew to great size. One story is told of a man wanting to buy five pounds of potatoes. The grocer humorously replied that he would not cut a potato in half for anyone.

Currently, the town of Palmer, Alaska, located just northeast of Wasilla, is home to many of the descendants of the settlers. Original structures from the colony are a part of the Alaska State Fairgrounds. Although not a booming success, the colony did help develop the Matanuska Valley into a primary agriculture region within Alaska.

In America's last frontier, the dream of opportunity and prosperity was a disappointment for many, but for others it was a hard won victory that set them on the road to success. Whether a success or failure, it must have been quite an adveture for the four families from Sheboygan County.

Above: Colonists arrive at Matanuska Valley, Alaska on May 10, 1935.

Below: Oversized Matanuska turnips grown on local farms in 1935.

Above: A permanent farm belonging to settlers in Alaska, 1940.

Son Of Former Falls Residents Dies In Alaska

George Charles Scheibl, 10-year-old son of Mr. and Mrs. Gust Scheibl, former Sheboygan Falls residents, died suddenly at the hospital in Palmer, Alaska, Monday, Feb. 8, at 12:25 a. m., Alaska time.

He had been ill one day with spinal meningitis. The second son of Mr. and Mrs. Scheibl, he was born Aug. 23, 1931, in Sheboygan Falls. The family moved to Alaska on May 13, 1935.

Survivors are the parents, three sisters and two brothers, Evelyn, Annabelle, Enolda, Allan and Franklin, all in Palmer, Alaska, and a grandmother, Mrs. Charles Goll of Sheboygan Falls.

A private funeral was held Wednesday, Feb. 10, in the Palmer Catholic church, the Rev. Fr. Snead officiating. A funeral mass will be read after the family is out of strict quarantine.

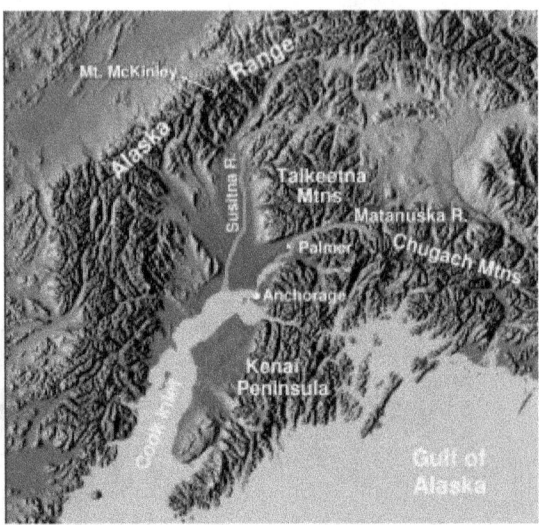

At left: Sheboygan Press article, February 1942, the Scheibl Family still lives in Alaska and suffers a tragedy.

Plymouth Rocks the County

October 13, 1946 is a day many in the county will never forget. Two unusual events rocked that placid Sunday afternoon in Plymouth. About 4:10pm a dreadful explosion rocked the area. It was almost immediately referred to as the Plymouth Bikini, a reference to the South Pacific atomic bomb tests.

Starting innocently enough, four Plymouth teenagers decided to spend their spare time out shooting sparrows. Robert Marth, Jerry Guenther, Daniel Gross and Wesley Steuerwald all of Plymouth drove south of town to the lane that was once the interurban line between Sheboygan and Plymouth. Located directly east of Cheeseville it's now Valley Road. In an open field just north of the lane stood an old contractor's shed on wheels owned by George Gardner aka Dynamite Bill. Lacking a skull and crossbones or DANGER warning, the trailer appeared harmless, but it housed "ditch" dynamite. An explosive more powerful than standard dynamite, it contained a higher percentage of nitroglycerine for a more robust blast.

One of the boys spotted a bird on the wheel of Bill's wagon. He fired once and missed, but the second shot was true. A slug from his .22 caliber rifle ripped into the side of the wagon. Over 1,000 pounds of dynamite went up in one boom. A cloud of dust streaked upward and the concussion spread for miles.

About 4 ½ times as powerful as gunpowder, dynamite is a mixture of sulphuric acid, nitric acid and glycerine. Reasonably stable at room temperature, it does its best work at 120 degrees Fahrenheit. Above 300 degrees it is liable to go off by itself. And when faced with a projectile traveling at roughly 900mph, the dynamite could only do one thing. Detonate!

The roof of the lads' car was peeled back from the force. At first, the kids thought the gas tank of the car exploded.

The blast broke windows and sheared off power poles in the area. The two boys seated in the rumble seat of the coupe were blown from the car, the driver of the car, leaped out as shattered glass from the windshield fell about him, and the young man who fired the shot was thrown to the ground, dazed. Clocks stopped. A chimney caved in on the north side of Plymouth and caused a fire. Pavement was covered with shattered glass.

People from all over Sheboygan County drove to Plymouth to see what had happened. Some even stood in the 12-foot deep, 20 foot diameter hole, that was gouged out by the blast.

Though detained by police neither Gardner nor the young man with the .22 were found to have violated any criminal law.

At nearly the same time, just six miles to the north, a single engine PT-19 army trainer airplane crashed to the ground near Johnsonville. Loren Hobbs and Harold Diers, both of Sheboygan, lost their lives when the plane nose-dived into a field on Alyerd Reinke's farm.

Flying low and circling a flock of seagulls the plane's motor sputtering wildly went into a spin. A split second later it crashed, crumbling accordion-like into the ground. The crash rocked the countryside.

Frighteningly, with gasoline everywhere, a mechanic used an acetylene torch to free one of the victims from the wreckage. Both young men were taken to the county morgue by Wittkopp Ambulance. Eye witnesses, Henry Laack and Carl Hirsch, provided police with details.

News accounts speculated whether the two events could be related, but no evidence of any investigation is seen later papers. Today, we know that bird strikes are a significant threat to flight safety, and have caused a number of accidents with human casualties.

Bird strikes happen most often during takeoff or landing, or during low altitude flight. Since 2000 nearly 500 planes have been damaged by collisions with birds according to the FAA. Some 166 of those planes had to make emergency landings bringing to mind US Airways 'miracle on the Hudson' guided by Captain Chesley Sullenberger where birds shut down two jet engines. The worst U.S. plane crash blamed on birds came on April 10, 1960, when an Eastern Airlines aircraft crashed into Boston Harbor, killing 62 passengers.

Difficult to prove nearly 70 years later, it is still likely the two events were connected. Following an explosion of such great magnitude from the dynamite cache, it is probable every bird in the county took flight. And if the twin-seater suddenly found itself surrounded by seagulls, disaster was likely.

Plymouth has seldom seen a day as memorable as this. Sorrowful and thrilling at the same time, it remains a favorite story to tell.

Above: Aftermath of the explosion on today's Valley Road in Plymouth.

Capelle's Appliance store on Mill Street cleans up after the explosion on October 13, 1946.

Above: The wreckage of the October 13, 1946 plane crash near Johnsonville.

At left: The gun and the sparrow shooter

Local Men Make History in Antarctica

Fifty-four years ago, on October 18, 1960, Sheboygan County made a bit of history in Antarctica.

First discovered in 1820 by the Russians and other seafaring explorers, the Earth's southernmost continent is surrounded by the Southern Ocean and is nearly twice the size of Australia. Mariners made early discoveries of coastal areas of Antarctica while sealing or whaling, but the exploration of the Antarctic interior began just over a century ago with the adventures of Scott, Byrd, Shackleton and Amundsen.

A forbidding land, about 98% of Antarctica is covered by a layer of ice that averages more than 1 mile in depth. It is the coldest, driest, and windiest continent on Earth. Improbably, it's considered a desert, receiving only about 8 inches of precipitation of any kind along the coast and far less inland. The mercury in Antarctica can dip as low as −129 °F, and although there is no indigenous population, up to 5,000 people reside throughout the year at scientific research stations scattered across the continent.

This is where Sheboygan County enters the picture. Three geographic features were named in honor of local men. The Kohler Range, is a span of mountains averaging 15,000-feet high, and named for Walter J. Kohler Sr. Helfert Nunatak, is a 6,900 foot peak was named for meteorologist, Norbert F. Helfert of Sheboygan. These three topographies are among a score of South Pole features named for people with a Wisconsin connection. Those honored tend to be the scientists who actually discovered the geographical feature, or academics who studied them or financial supporters who funded exploratory expeditions.

The Kohler Range was named by Rear Admiral Richard E. Byrd for Kohler, a former governor of Wisconsin (1929-1931). This range of mountains was first seen on February 24, 1940 by Byrd and other members of the United States Antarctic service expedition. Kohler Sr., also known as 'The Flying Governor' was a financial supporter of the Byrd Antarctic expedition of 1933-1935. A flying enthusiast, he furnished the Barkley-Grow seaplane from which the range was discovered.

A supplier of Kohler generators reports that five Kohler "electric plants" or generators were donated for Byrd's first Antarctic trip in 1929. They remained unused during that foray, but five years later after drying out the spark plugs and priming the engines, they powered up and were used for the second expedition in 1934. During this expedition Byrd spent six months at a remote outpost during

Antarctica's winter, relying on the generators for his sole source of power for heat, light and communications.

The Kohler Glacier, a second geographical feature, bisects the Kohler Range and flows northward into the Dotson Ice Shelf.

The third entity, Helfert Nunatak, is a peak named for Norbert F. Helfert, a 1954 grad of Sheboygan North High School and a student of meteorology at Penn State. Helfert Nunatak stands near the Sentinel Mountains. Norbert spent nearly a year in the Antarctic in 1957 as a civilian observer for the U.S. Weather Bureau during its Geophysical Year scientific undertakings. During his summer vacations he was employed by the U.S. Weather Bureau in Milwaukee. His duties during his year in Antarctica involved making weather, temperature and humidity observations on the earth's surface and in the upper air above Byrd Station.

Antarctica is owned by no one. Although a few nations, including Australia, Argentina, and the United Kingdom, have tried to lay claim to it over the years, it remains free of government and ownership. In 1959, the Antarctic Treaty (ATS) was drafted, designating the land as "a natural reserve, devoted to peace and science." Fifty nations have signed to date. The treaty prohibits military activities and mineral mining, prohibits nuclear explosions and nuclear waste disposal, supports scientific research, and protects the continent's environment.

Naming is an interesting process at the South Pole since there are no permanent settlements or residents. Most major features of Antarctica have been discovered and mapped, but a vast number of secondary features continue to be only partially delineated and remain unnamed.

Decisions on Antarctic names are based on a first come, first served basis. The names must be appropriate and discernable; they must have a legitimate connection to something or someone important to Antarctica. Over the last thirty years the U.S. Geological Survey has mapped over 870,000 square miles of the continent previously unmapped. GPS must be a wonderful addition to a cartographer's toolbox.

What was once an exotic adventure, a trip to Antarctica, has become something much more routine. Nearly 5,000 scientists from 25 countries work there each year. In addition, the emergence of eco-tourism has resulted in large numbers of people visiting Antarctica – more than 45,000 tourists in the peak year of 2007-2008.

So, pick up a map, or Google Antarctica. Find the Kohler Range and glacier. Find Helfert Nunatak, and enjoy the fact that you know the rest of the story.

At left:
Norbert Helfert, 1954 Graduate of Sheboygan North High School and meteorologist for the U.S. Weather Bureau.

At right:
Governor Walter J. Kohler Sr.

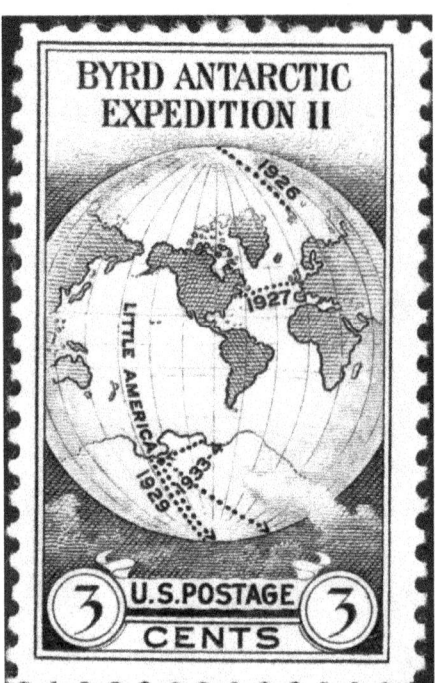

At left: Byrd Expedition U.S. postage stamp

Below: Map of Antarctica,

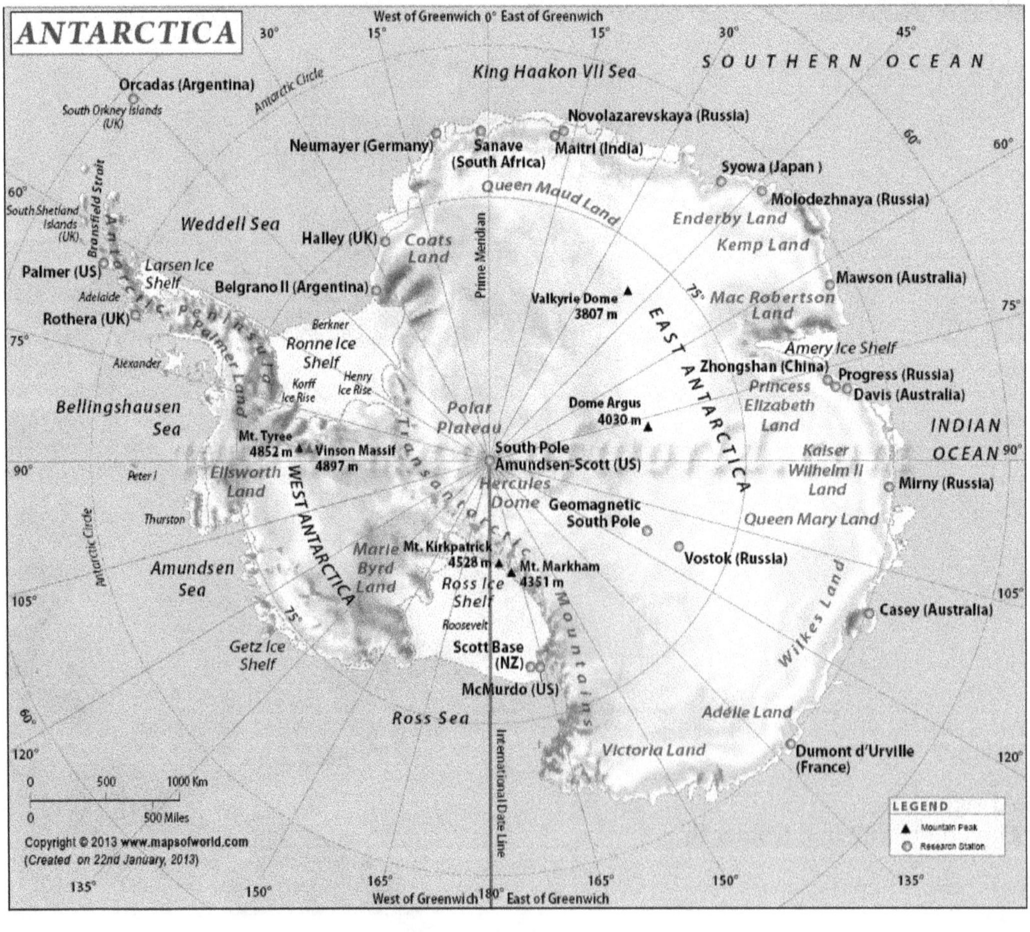

Above: Barkley-Grow seaplane

Below: Antarctic expedition equipment being unloaded

An Uncommon Friendship

Forty-two years ago this October 24th John Roosevelt Robinson passed away at the age of 53 and with his death a most uncommon friendship came to an end.

Jackie Robinson, as we know him, is famous for his stellar baseball career, but should also be remembered for his place in the early civil rights movement, his common decency and his singular friendship with a Sheboygan boy, Ron Rabinovitz.

Robinson was born in 1919 and grew up in California where he was an accomplished athlete lettering in four sports at UCLA with hopes of something bigger. But, WWII stepped in and when he entered the U.S. Army in 1942, it was still a segregated institution. Little known is an episode where Robinson faced court-martial at Ft. Hood in 1944 for refusing an order to move to the back of a bus. He was cleared only after it was found that the order from a superior was a violation of Army regulations. Not until 1948 did a presidential mandate from Harry Truman finally desegregate the military.

After leaving the army Robinson joined the Kansas City Monarchs, a Negro League team where he met Branch Rickey, the general manager of the Dodgers, who would forever change his life and the sport of baseball by demanding change.

Both men knew the hazards, that the first to run the gauntlet of integration would have to withstand racial abuse and insults. Rickey worked with Robinson to be certain Jackie was up to the job. Could he stand up to the taunts and jeers? Could he avoid open confrontation with detractors? The first black baseball player to cross the "color line" would be subjected to intense public scrutiny.

Jackie's skills on the field, his integrity, and his deep devotion to family were necessary components to cross that line, yet criticism came from all sides. Black players at the time felt Jack was not the best player. Josh Gibson and Satchel Paige were perhaps more talented, yet Rickey felt Robinson was a better candidate

On October 23, 1945, Rickey signed Robinson to play on the Montreal Royals, a Dodger's farm team. Robinson led that league in batting average in 1946 and was brought up to play for Brooklyn in 1947.

He was an immediate success on the field. Leading the National League in stolen bases, he was chosen Rookie of the Year. In 1949 he won the batting championship with a .342 average and was voted the league's Most Valuable Player (MVP).

After a successful season with the minor league Montreal Royals in 1946, Robinson officially broke the major league color barrier when he put on a Dodgers uniform, number 42, in April 1947.

In 1952, Brooklyn met Sheboygan when David Rabinovitz, a local attorney and great admirer of the Dodgers for their policy on integration, wrote a quick note to Robinson on behalf of his 7 year old son, Ronnie, another Dodgers' devotee.

Ronnie Rabinovitz received an autographed picture and an invitation to meet Robinson when the Dodgers were in town. So, the next time the Braves played in Milwaukee, the Rabinovitz family was there. Robinson remembered the polite communication on legal letterhead from a kid who spoke of his enthusiasm for the team. A bond between the two formed quickly. They talked honestly and openly like old friends.

Even after Robinson retired in 1956, the friendship continued. Ronnie corresponded with Robinson from 1952 to 1962, crafting handwritten letters that talked about everything and yet nothing, from race issues to weight problems and politics to sports.

Robinson's kindness provided lasting memories for Ronnie; Jackie hit a home run on Ron's 10th birthday, waving to the boy in the stands. When Ron graduated from Sheboygan North High School in 1963, he received a telegram saying, "Always proud of your achievements; continued good luck. Always, Jackie."

Sadly, bigotry also followed Robinson to Sheboygan. In 1960, after speaking at an event for the National Conference of Christians and Jews, someone spray-painted a vicious message with the "n word" on the wall of Rabinovitz's law office.

Robinson's lifetime batting average was .311, and he led the Dodgers to six championships and one World Series victory. Perhaps his greatest skill was in stealing bases. Or perhaps it was his character and integrity.

Ron Rabinovitz is determined that his friend, Jackie Robinson, is not forgotten. The two were so different, yet they found something in each other that brought comfort to each of them.

Rabinovitz still brings his message to school children and is ever grateful for his uncommon friendship with Jackie Robinson, an athlete who made an enduring impact on one child's life, and a man who forced a watershed moment in America's history.

At left: Jackie Robinson and Ronnie Rabinovitz, his greatest fan.

At left: Correspondence and photos from Jackie Robinson.

The Bubbler, Debunking the Myth

This year in the United States alone, more than 25 billion bottles of water will be consumed by thirsty Americans. But, as little as twenty years ago drinking water came from very different sources, the kitchen faucet, the water cooler, a thermos or when in public, from our parochial favorite, the bubbler.

The modern American drinking fountain was crafted independently by two men at much the same time; in 1909 by Luther Haws in Berkeley, California and Halsey Taylor in 1912 in Warren, Ohio. Halsey Taylor's father died of typhoid fever caused by contaminated public drinking water. His father's death motivated him to invent the drinking water fountain to provide safer drinking water. Luther Haws was disturbed by school children drinking water out of a common tin cup. Haws also feared there was a health hazard in the way the kids were sharing their water supply.

Now, how does Sheboygan County come into the drinking water conversation? Well, it involves Kohler Co. and the bubbler. Perhaps not quite an urban myth because it's neither horrific nor humorous, but equally false is the story that our very own Kohler Co. invented and holds the patent for a Wisconsin favorite, the bubbler.

The Internet abounds with reports that claim the Bubbler is a trademarked name for a product designed in 1888 by a man named Harlan Huckleby who worked for Kohler Water Works, now Kohler Co. and that Kohler actually patented the invention and trademarked the name. As the story goes, the original Bubbler shot water one inch straight into the air, creating the bubbling phenomenon that gave the product its name.

Interesting story, but so very wrong. It is time to debunk the Kohler bubbler story. Number one, no evidence can be found of a company called the Kohler Water Works, and it certainly was not a predecessor of Kohler. Kohler Co. did not exist in its present form and location until about 1900 and Kohler village did not exist until 1912 when it was incorporated.

After consulting the archivist at Kohler Co. we find that the company has never claimed to having invented the bubbler, nor does it hold the patent. They've searched patent records and their own records to no avail. The same goes for the employee, Harlan Hucklebee. There is no record of Harlan working at Kohler Co.

But the company does make great bubblers, producing white, enameled cast iron, pedestal drinking fountains since about 1900. Vitreous china pedestal and wall-hung fountains were first offered around 1927. These fixtures were fitted with brass valves described as continuous flow bubblers or bubbling valves. However, Kohler did not manufacture these brass pieces themselves until 1926.

So, where did the urban myth begin? We may never know.

But, we do know that Wisconsin is one of the few places on earth that calls the drinking fountain a bubbler. It is a wonderful regional colloquialism peculiar to ourselves.

One possibility when it comes to the origin of the term 'bubbler' begins in our local schools. Wisconsin was filled with one-room schools in the late 19th Century, and each school had a pretty standard set of furniture and equipment including portraits of George Washington and Abraham Lincoln, blackboards, the old pot-bellied stove, maybe a globe and some type of container for drinking water. One container frequently used was the Red Wing Stoneware Company's ceramic water cooler or water 'bubbler' made as early as 1877. They came in three-gallon and five-gallon sizes and were prized possessions of schools.

In District #12, Town of Holland's Lakeview School the water cooler was always called the bubbler by students and teachers. The cooler, filled from the top, was emptied by using the spigot at the bottom. The air bubbles moving from the bottom to the top when the spigot was pushed caused the bubble noise. Hence, the name "bubbler." Some Red Wing water coolers actually had attachments called 'bubblers.'

When talking to former one-room school students the bubbler is always fondly mentioned. It was exciting new technology for its time. Town of Mitchell students in three schools loved their bubblers. Spring Farm School students reported that "drinking water was drawn from an outdoor well and stored in a bubbler" as early as 1900. One memory from a Payne School student reported, "We would hurry to the bubbler to get a drink of water, and sometimes the bubbler would be dry. Someone had forgotten to fill it." Rathbun School even had a specific water carrier, "Walter Knauer, brought fresh water every morning for the bubbler. All awaited his coming."

Bubblers could even be fashionable. A drinking fountain for horses and a bubbler for people was erected at the corner of Jefferson Avenue and 7th Street as a memorial to the late James Mead and marked the location where he dropped dead in September of 1891. Mead left a gift from his estate which was the basis for funding of Mead Public Library.

The true origin of the word may remain a mystery, but we do know that before bottled water there was the drinking fountain, and in Wisconsin there was, and is, the bubbler.

At left: The Town of Holland Lakeview School's bubbler. The water cooler was usually called the bubbler by students and teachers in town of Holland school rooms. The cooler needed to be filled from the top and was emptied by using the spigot at the bottom. The water would be drunk from the common dipper. The air bubbles moving from the bottom to the top when the spigot was pushed caused the bubble noise. Hence, the name "bubbler."

At left: A Redwing water cooler with bubbler attachment.

Above: The drinking fountain for horses and people erected at the corner of Jefferson Avenue and 7th Street as a memorial to James Mead and marked the location where he dropped dead in September of 1891. Mead left a gift from his estate which was the basis for funding for Mead Public Library.

At right: A pictorial timeline of some of Kohler Company's drinking fountains.

Above: Hika School, Centerville showing students lining up for a drink from the artesian well fitted with a bubbler attachment. Circa 1920.

At left: At the 1874 organizing convention of the National Woman's Christian Temperance Union, the members were urged to erect drinking fountains in their towns so that men could get a drink of water without entering saloons and staying for stronger drinks. The drinking fountains that were erected often offered a place for horses to drink, another place for dogs, and of course, a place for humans to drink. At left is an iconic Benson Bubbler with four bowls in Portland, Oregon.

Friday Night Fish Fries
Sheboygan County Tradition Continues

The Friday night fish fry, long a Wisconsin tradition, first appeared in 1920 in Appleton, according to Chris Martell in his August 2002 article, *Talk Aims to Feed Curiosity About Fish Fry Tradition*, published in the Wisconsin State Journal.

During Prohibition, which began in January of 1920, traditional taverns and bars had to find new ways to conduct business. Many taverns became soda fountains or ice cream shoppes during President Hoover's *Noble Experiment,* but others started serving fish fries on Fridays, the day men traditionally were paid for their week's work.

Although Prohibition was not officially repealed until December 5, 1933, on April 7th of 1933 the Cullen-Harrison bill allowed breweries to produce beer with 3.2% alcohol content. The tavern was back. Once prohibition was rescinded, neighborhood watering holes began offering inexpensive fish fries for as little as 10 cents. The tavern keepers hoped to make up for the low cost of the fish fries by selling more beer.

The popularity of the Friday night fish fry tradition in Sheboygan County was fueled by a number of factors in addition to the end of Prohibition. There was 1) the need to escape the dreariness which came from the hard-time Depression years, 2) the Germanic tradition of *Gemuetlikeit* , 3) the Catholic Church's ban on eating meat on Fridays, and 4) the availability of fresh fish from nearby Lake Michigan.

The Great Depression took its toll on the morale of all Americans. Envision fish fries in Sheboygan County years ago and your mind will likely picture checkered tablecloths, steins of foam-flecked beer and plates loaded with French fries, coleslaw, warm bread and fillets of Lake Michigan perch. Gathering at a bar with one's friends for a cheap meal and good conversation went a long way toward lifting the spirits of everyone.

Sheboygan's Germanic sense of Gemuetlikeit meshed well with the community atmosphere of an evening meal held in a public forum with friends rather than just family.

In the 1930s the Catholic Church reaffirmed that Fridays during Lent be meatless days for its members in observance of Christ's crucifixion on the cross. Abstaining from meat goes back to the fourth century, but Pope Pius the IX felt that

Catholics were becoming too lax in their observance of the custom, so he issued an encyclical urging this penance.

Seemingly unlimited quantities of fresh and tasty lake perch, harvested just off shore of Sheboygan, also made the Friday fish fry possible.

Tavern owners soon took advantage of these factors and began offering Friday night fish dinners. Catholics responded enthusiastically, but Sheboygan's large Protestant population soon joined in, together creating a wonderful Friday night tradition.

The Schwarz Fish Co., founded in 1911 by Herman and William Schwarz, started with just three employees concentrating on the production of high-quality smoked fish. The Schwarz operation was housed in a small building on the banks of the Sheboygan River, near the site of the Riverside plant of the Wisconsin Power and Light Company on the north side of the Sheboygan River.

Organized as a corporation in 1946, the firm employed about 30 people and served a 12-county area throughout northeastern Wisconsin. At that time the company processed between two and three million tons of fish annually, ranking it as one of the largest fish companies in the state of Wisconsin. Company trucks made weekly trips to Canada and Lake Erie to pick up fresh fish for processing at the local plant.

More than eight tons of fish were brought to Sheboygan each week by truck from Lake Winnipeg in Canada. Lake Michigan chubs were supplied by commercial fishermen in Sheboygan and Two Rivers.

Schwarz Fish Co. has supplied many of Sheboygan County's perch-serving eateries over the years. But so have some individual fishing sportsmen in earlier years. One of them lived across the street from me and my wife in the mid-1950s. He was Roman Kleinschmidt, a member at Holy Name Catholic Church, 807 Superior Avenue in Sheboygan.

Kleinschmidt had his own boat and fish nets docked below the bluff at the east end of Blackstock Avenue. On a part-time basis, he netted a lot of perch which he sold to local taverns or passed along to relatives and friends, according to his daughter Marilyn (Kleinschmidt) Damkot. Damkot's father was employed full-time at the Garton Toy Company for more than 35 years. He died in 1984.

Damkot also said that her father's fisherman friend, "Dynamite" Jeske--she didn't know his real first name--also sold the perch that he caught to local tavern owners. Presumably, there were other local fishermen who did the same.

Today's fish fries have changed just a bit from the 1930s and 1940s. Fish fries served in taverns in the 1940s were inexpensive---10 cents and later, 25 cents. Currently, they're in the $9-$12 range. Restaurant prices are a bit higher.

Today's fish fries are no longer served on tables with checkered table cloths and they are not limited to Friday nights during Lent. And the fish entree is no longer just Lake Michigan perch. But, since there are 14 Catholic churches in Sheboygan County today, six of them in the city of Sheboygan and eight of them in the outlying areas of the count the fish fry is alive and well. Where else, but in Wisconsin, would taverns and churches find a common ground---"Church-goers eating fish once a week---on Fridays at neighborhood taverns or elsewhere during the Lenten season?

Two of the county's Catholic churches still sponsor Friday night fish fries, both as fund raisers for special projects. St. Peter Claver in Sheboygan has an ambitious schedule. It conducts six fries a year, one on the first Fridays in January, February, March, April, May and December.

Al and Penny Awe, St. Peter Claver church members, started the fish fry event at the church in 1982. Mark and Marge Verhelst also members at the church, are the current chairs.

The Verhelsts enlisted the expert assistance of the late Mary Susha Ziegenhorn who owned and operated Zieggy's Tavern, one of Sheboygan's popular fish fry destinations for many years.

St. John the Baptist in Plymouth has been serving a variety of fish fries since 1988. Angie Jacoby organized the Plymouth church's first fish fry event. Gloria

Friday night fish fries have been held at St. John the Baptist Catholic Church in Plymouth for 20 years. And they're still popular.

Meyer took over from Jacoby for the next four years. A trio of church members---Pat Kulow, Kris Wimmler and Josette Switter---was in charge of the 2008 event. The menu included perch, noodles, applesauce, coleslaw, bread and dessert for $9 a plate.

One of Sheboygan's oldest taverns featuring Friday night fish fries is Ziggy's Bar and Grill. Previously known as Suscha's Tavern, Zieggy's was last year named the "Best Place in Sheboygan County for a Friday Night Fish Fry," The annual poll is sponsored by the *Sheboygan Press*. Zieggy's also won the "best" honor several times in the previous polls.

The best Friday night Fish Fry in the county in 2008, according to the poll was the Scenic Bar and Restaurant, also in Sheboygan. In another category, Schwarz Fish Market, also in Sheboygan, was selected the best seafood provider.

Mary Suscha Ziegenhorn's parents owned the popular bar and grill before their daughter and her husband Maurice "Babe" Ziegenhorn took it over in 1955. Mary's cooking was credited for the tavern's long success; she served over 600 fish fry meals from a very small kitchen. Local fishermen often brought her the perch they caught and she cooked them for Friday fish luncheons. The lunch was always free to customers, she told friends, because she got the perch free of charge.

This Schwarz Fish Company truck was used to deliver shrimp, lobster tails, ocean fish and a variety of fresh fish to grocers, butchers and saloons locally and throughout the state in 1925.

This article was written and contributed by Robert Spatt in 2008.

The Tale of Two Cows, $5 and A Long Walk in the Mid-1800s

If you were a farmer in Sheboygan County sometime in the mid-1800s would you have walked to Milwaukee---two trips totaling an estimated 280 miles---for five dollars? Carl Schulz, a farmer from the Town of Herman did.

He walked there to buy a cow . . . two cows as it turned out. It's a true story, an interesting and fascinating story, but one that prompts a number of unanswered questions about Schulz's adventurous journey. The following story, therefore, includes many assumptions---based on local history---in addition to the facts actually known. The story is about members of the Stoll and Schulz families, the cows and two-140-mile trips to Milwaukee that took place in the late 1850s or early 1860s.

Friedrich and Martha Stoll and their three children---Louise, Heinrich and Louis---immigrated to America from Germany in 1850. They came from Brockhorst, Holstein, Germany, aboard a sailing ship named the Marie Fredericke. It is recorded that the ship docked in Quebec, Canada, in April of that same year. Louis, eight months old, did not survive the stormy trip and was buried at sea.

Why or how the Stolls came to the Town of Herman in northern Sheboygan County from Quebec is not known, except that there were many other German settlers already located there. A more important reason, however, might have been that land agents were offering 40 acres of land in the Town of Herman for as little as $1.25. The agents also reminded immigrants that Wisconsin had recently (on May 29, 1848) become the 30th state in the growing Union.

The Stolls purchased their 40 acres, sight unseen. Friedrich wanted to build a gristmill on his property but the river he expected and was promised by the land agent---turned out to be a small creek. The land was also densely wooded.

About that same time, another German immigrant, Carl Schulz, came to the Town of Herman, where he met and in 1857 married Stoll's daughter, Louise. Carl and Louise bought the 40-acre plot from his father-in-law and began clearing some of the land to build a log house and plant some crops. Schulz also wanted some farm animals, especially a cow to provide enough milk for the family.

Sometime during the early 1860s, Carl Schulz walked to Milwaukee where he purchased his cow, probably a solid red-brown Devon, a Durham, or a Devon-Durham-cross breed, all dual purpose animals. The breeds, known as superior milking cows, were popular on farms in the mid-19th century.

After walking back to his farm from Milwaukee, Schulz's neighbor offered to buy the cow for $5 more than Schulz paid for it. Schulz accepted the offer and promptly walked back to Milwaukee, purchased another cow and led it back home.

Unfortunately, other details about the trips and transactions are unknown. Based on historical research, we can only assume what really happened. Some of questions still to be answered include:

Where in Milwaukee did Carl Schulz buy his cows? At what cost? Maybe he bought them from a Milwaukee area farmer, maybe not. Research has not resulted in any information about a specific source where cows could have been purchased in Milwaukee and what they would have cost. Some farmers at that time often bought off-spring cows from their neighbors. Schulz did not. He definitely walked to Milwaukee to buy his cow, according to family members.

In a book authored by Alice E. Smith, entitled "The History of Wisconsin," there is a reference to the Milwaukee system for agricultural operations, namely raising grains, fruits, roots and other agricultural crops; there were no references to dealing with cattle sales.

As an aside, the society also noted that there were 183,433 cattle in the state by 1849: 64,339 of them milk cows, 42,801 oxen and 76,293 "other cattle." Obviously, cattle were not in short supply then. It was recorded elsewhere that farm animals and farm equipment were available for purchase in the Green Bay area.

Jerry Apps, professor emeritus of agriculture at the University of Wisconsin, has written many books on rural history and country life. Apps was born and raised on a Wisconsin farm. He suggests that Schulz may have obtained his cows at the Milwaukee Stockyards.

"I remember going there as a kid with dairy cattle. Most of the cows then were sold to the packing houses but I would guess that in the early days they were sold to farmers who wanted one as well," Apps said.

Don Klemme grew up on a farm in the Town of Sheboygan Falls. Klemme recalls that his father, Herbert, bought seven Holstein heifers in Milwaukee for $100 in 1931 but doesn't know where his father purchased them. A retired teacher, Klemme taught agricultural and biology classes at Howards Grove High School from 1960-90.

What route did Carl Schulz take to and from Milwaukee? There were two early roads in Sheboygan County, one extending north and south, linking Fort Howard in Green Bay with Fort Dearborn in Chicago. The other ran east and west, connecting Sheboygan with Fond du Lac. It continued on to western Wisconsin. Both were military roads built by the United States government.

Construction on the Green Bay Road, also known as the Green Bay Ethnic Trail, began in 1835. The Green Bay Road was 30 feet wide. All trees in its path, less than 12 inches wide, were cut to within six inches of the ground. Those over 12 inches wide were cut to within one foot of the ground. Stumps were left in the ground to rot, rather than removed from the right-or-way. As a result, they were a hazard to anyone on horseback or anyone using a horse-drawn a wagon. Bridges were built across rivers and most streams. Small streams were filled in with heavy logs and topped with a handrail. The road was crude and the poor conditions limited its use.

Initially, the Green Bay Road served as a communications and a supply link between Fort Howard and Fort Dearborn. Early wayside hotels were constructed along the road. Taverns and inns were other options for travelers. The Green Bay Road was used for about 20 years, until 1860. More modern roads---some of which were constructed along or near the original alignment---eventually replaced the old military roads. Parts of today's Wisconsin highways 42 and 32 and even Interstate 43 are the route of the old Green Bay Road.

The Schulz family homestead is located just east of Ada, a short distance from the current Highways 32 and 42. Therefore, it can be assumed that this was Carl Schulz's travel route to and from Milwaukee. The Green Bay road passed through Howards Grove, Sheboygan Falls, Gibbsville and Cedar Grove in Sheboygan County, and was close to the Port Washington, Saukville and Brown Deer communities in Ozaukee and Washington counties.

When did Carl Schulz go to Milwaukee? This may be the easiest question to answer: The best weather would normally be in the spring, summer or fall. Who would want to make a trip like that in winter time? Historians, however, claim that there was more travel, at least by horseback or wagon, on the Green Bay Road in the winter because the road often was soft and muddy due to rain in the warmer seasons.

How long did the trips take him? A difficult question to answer for obvious reasons. There are estimates that vary from several days to several weeks. It is reasonable to expect that Schulz walked faster alone than he did with the cows. Another factor to consider is that a cow can probably walk about two or three miles in an hour.

There also is a somewhat comparative travel experience that may provide some insight for answering the question. A Sauk County Historical Society member writing in the May 5, 1914 issue of the Baraboo Daily News, commented that ". . . hauling wheat in horse- or oxen-drawn wagons from Baraboo on another military road to Milwaukee (roughly about 125 miles) was a two-to-three weeks trip in the 1850s." This might be a case of comparing apples and oranges but it gives some idea of travel time on military roads in those years.

The writer went on to say: "No (Baraboo settler) ever indulged in the luxury of stopping at a hotel or inn unless compelled to do so by sickness or a bad storm. Camping out was an alternative."

Friedrich and Martha Stoll

Carl and Louise Schultz

An 1860s drawing of a Durham bull., one of the earliest cows found in Wisconsin.

Did Schulz stop along the way to eat and sleep, and if so, where? Schulz probably did. There were inns and hotels along the Green Bay Trail in Sheboygan, Ozaukee and Washington counties. Even other farm owners Schulz passed during his trips might have been willing to put him up for a night. He was known to be active in the Schwarzwald (Evangelical and Reformed) church near his farm. There were a number of small churches along the route that might have been willing to give a churchman refuge. Staying with friends or relatives who lived along the Green Bay trail was another possibility.

Edmund Schulz, now 84, who owns the Schulz family homestead in the Town of Herman, said his father, Albert Schulz, in 1936 told him the story about Edmund's grandfather, Carl Schulz, walking to Milwaukee to buy the cows. Edmund was 14 years old at the time.

One of the reasons the father and his young son probably never discussed the story again---is that Albert Schulz was fatally injured on Sept. 4, 1936, when two sticks of dynamite that had failed to explode went off as he was inspecting them. He and a hired man had been blasting stumps in a field at the time of the accident. Albert Schulz was 59 years old when he died.

There's probably a lesson here, one we've all experienced at one time or another: If you want to know something about your family's history, ask your questions before it's too late!

From the
Western People, Ballina, County Mayo, Ireland
Saturday, October 5, 1957
The Irish in Wisconsin- Interesting Vacation Story-

How Mayo Contributed to American History.

This unusual vacation story sent to the *Western People* newspaper by a former Kiltimagh (Mayo) man seemed to have some news appeal and we could not resist giving it the title, "The Irish in Wisconsin".

It was vacation time for Jim Keegan and family of Chicago, so they decided to spend it in the Kettle Moraine State Forest in Wisconsin. This is a state controlled natural forest of beautiful trees veined with miles of auto trails and dotted with many lovely lakes. It is a vacationer's dream spot. Residing at Forest Lake (just across the border into Fond du Lac County), Mr. Keegan decided during the first week of a three weeks August vacation to tour one of the auto trails. After wandering as far a Greenbush he made his way back toward home along the back country roads where the family noticed a small, neat cemetery with many Irish names on the tombstones. This is where the story begins- BACK IN MAYO- Mr. Keegan knew he was in a part of Wisconsin which was supposed to be mostly German and Polish. Curiosity got the better of him so he decided to go into the cemetery and look around. After reading a few of the inscriptions he thought he was back in County Mayo. He read further, name after name, date after date. The names captivated him so much that he copied them just as they were inscribed. We name some of them in alphabetical order:

James Brown born Coneil, County Mayo 1810, died April 8, 1897; Michael Collins, born Crossmolina, County Mayo, 1820, died February 16, 1867; Owen Cummings, born County Mayo October 23, 1831, died April 4, 1923, Anthony Gallagher born County Mayo, 1802, died August 13, 1868; Patrick Gerity, born parish of Kilmeena, County Mayo, 1819, died July 8, 1889; Mary Gilboy, born Ardagh, County Mayo 1797, died May 2, 1885, Daniel Heraty, born Aughagower, County Mayo, 1802, died February 19, 1875; Hannah Howley Foley born County Mayo, 1795, died January 26, 1893; James Hughes born Parish of Lacken, County Mayo, 1794, died January 19, 1864; Thomas Jordan born County Mayo April 10, 1814, died March 14, 1892; James Lavell born County Mayo 1800, died March

13, 1880; Michael Mugan born Islandeady, County Mayo, 1818, died November 1, 1876; Dominick Manley born Breachy, County Mayo, May 1, 1799, died February 18, 1868; Michael McDonnell born Killmore, County Mayo 1799, died August 19, 1882; Michal Nolan born Westport, County Mayo 1838, died May 9, 1874; Patrick Reddington born County Mayo, November 5, 1816, died May 15, 1891.

While most of the names were of County Mayo, other countries were also listed- the Slatterys of Tipperary, Dwyers of Cork, Powers of Kilkenny, Caufields and Burkes of Galway, Gahagans of Roscommon, Lindsays of Antrim, Rooneys of Sligo, Gaynors of Westmeath, McGarveys of Cavan, O'Briens of Waterford, Murpheys of Cork and Reillys of Louth.

In a true sense of the word, it was an Irish cemetery in a foreign land, resting under well-kept lawns of green. We know these pioneers of the central U.S.A. are close to the hearts of the people in Ireland.

St. Michael's Church and Cemetery, Town of Mitchell

Joe Reilly, son of James and Mary Norris Reilly, James Hanahan, son of Martin and Alice Lavelle Hanahan and James Reilly, son of James and Mary Norris Reilly

www.ingramcontent.com/pod-product-compliance
Lightning Source LLC
Chambersburg PA
CBHW080339170426
43194CB00014B/2627